New Directions for Community Colleges

Arthur M. Cohen
EDITOR-IN-CHIEF

Caroline Q. Durdella
Nathan R. Durdella
ASSOCIATE EDITORS

Amy Fara Edwards
MANAGING EDITOR

Preparing a STEM Workforce through Career-Technical Education

Dimitra Jackson Smith
Soko Starobin
EDITORS

Number 178 • Summer 2017
Jossey-Bass
San Francisco

Preparing a STEM Workforce through Career-Technical Education
Dimitra Jackson Smith, Soko Starobin (eds.)
New Directions for Community Colleges, no. 178

Editor-in-Chief: *Arthur M. Cohen*
Associate Editors: *Caroline Q. Durdella, Nathan R. Durdella*
Managing Editor: *Amy Fara Edwards*

New Directions for Community Colleges, (ISSN 0194-3081; Online ISSN: 1536-0733), is published quarterly by Wiley Subscription Services, Inc., a Wiley Company, 111 River St., Hoboken, NJ 07030-5774 USA.

Postmaster: Send all address changes to *New Directions for Community Colleges*, John Wiley & Sons Inc., C/O The Sheridan Press, PO Box 465, Hanover, PA 17331 USA.

Information for subscribers

New Directions for Community Colleges is published in 4 issues per year. Institutional subscription prices for 2017 are:

Print & Online: US$454 (US), US$507 (Canada & Mexico), US$554 (Rest of World), €363 (Europe), £285 (UK). Prices are exclusive of tax. Asia-Pacific GST, Canadian GST/HST and European VAT will be applied at the appropriate rates. For more information on current tax rates, please go to www.wileyonlinelibrary.com/tax-vat. The price includes online access to the current and all online backfiles to January 1st 2013, where available. For other pricing options, including access information and terms and conditions, please visit www.wileyonlinelibrary.com/access.

Delivery Terms and Legal Title

Where the subscription price includes print issues and delivery is to the recipient's address, delivery terms are **Delivered at Place (DAP)**; the recipient is responsible for paying any import duty or taxes. Title to all issues transfers FOB our shipping point, freight prepaid. We will endeavour to fulfil claims for missing or damaged copies within six months of publication, within our reasonable discretion and subject to availability.

Back issues: Single issues from current and recent volumes are available at the current single issue price from cs-journals@wiley.com.

Disclaimer

The Publisher and Editors cannot be held responsible for errors or any consequences arising from the use of information contained in this journal; the views and opinions expressed do not necessarily reflect those of the Publisher and Editors, neither does the publication of advertisements constitute any endorsement by the Publisher and Editors of the products advertised.

Publisher: New Directions for Community Colleges is published by Wiley Periodicals, Inc., 350 Main St., Malden, MA 02148–5020.

Journal Customer Services: For ordering information, claims and any enquiry concerning your journal subscription please go to www.wileycustomerhelp.com/ask or contact your nearest office.
Americas: Email: cs-journals@wiley.com; Tel: +1 781 388 8598 or +1 800 835 6770 (toll free in the USA & Canada).
Europe, Middle East and Africa: Email: cs-journals@wiley.com; Tel: +44 (0) 1865 778315.
Asia Pacific: Email: cs-journals@wiley.com; Tel: +65 6511 8000.
Japan: For Japanese speaking support, Email: cs-japan@wiley.com.
Visit our Online Customer Help available in 7 languages at www.wileycustomerhelp.com/ask

Production Editor: Shreya Srivastava (email: shsrivsata@wiley.com).

Wiley's Corporate Citizenship initiative seeks to address the environmental, social, economic, and ethical challenges faced in our business and which are important to our diverse stakeholder groups. Since launching the initiative, we have focused on sharing our content with those in need, enhancing community philanthropy, reducing our carbon impact, creating global guidelines and best practices for paper use, establishing a vendor code of ethics, and engaging our colleagues and other stakeholders in our efforts. Follow our progress at www.wiley.com/go/citizenship

View this journal online at wileyonlinelibrary.com/journal/cc

Wiley is a founding member of the UN-backed HINARI, AGORA, and OARE initiatives. They are now collectively known as Research4Life, making online scientific content available free or at nominal cost to researchers in developing countries. Please visit Wiley's Content Access – Corporate Citizenship site: http://www.wiley.com/WileyCDA/Section/id-390082.html

Printed in the USA by The Sheridan Group.

Address for Editorial Correspondence should be sent to the Editor-in-Chief, Arthur M. Cohen, at 1749 Mandeville Lane, Los Angeles, CA 90049. All manuscripts receive anonymous reviews by external referees.

Abstracting and Indexing Services

The Journal is indexed by Academic Search Alumni Edition (EBSCO Publishing); Education Index/Abstracts (EBSCO Publishing); ERA: Educational Research Abstracts Online (T&F); ERIC: Educational Resources Information Center (CSC); MLA International Bibliography (MLA).

Cover design: Wiley
Cover Images: © Lava 4 images | Shutterstock

For submission instructions, subscription and all other information visit: wileyonlinelibrary.com/journal/cc

CONTENTS

Editors' Notes

Preparing a competent and prepared science, technology, engineering, and mathematics (STEM) workforce is, no doubt, at the forefront within all sectors including K–12 academic institutions, community colleges, colleges, and universities, as well as within business and industry. In fact, "over the past decade, concern has been growing among government agencies, national organizations and private industry over the declining state of STEM education in the United States" (STEM Connector, 2014, p. 4). Coupled with this concern are the Bureau of Labor Statistics projections regarding the increase of newly created jobs and the retirement of baby boomers that will create more than 3 million job openings in STEM by 2018 (Lacey & Wright, 2009). Career and technical education (CTE) programs are beneficial to high school students, college students, adults, and the economy and business. According to the Reeve (2013), CTE programs are designed to "prepare youth and adults for a wide range of high-wage, high-skill, high-demand careers" (para. 1). These programs have proven to be beneficial in preparing students on the postsecondary and adult level for career opportunities that will allow them to be contributing citizens by providing real-world, hands-on learning opportunities related to STEM (ACTE). The benefits of these programs are reflected in the graduation rate of high school students concentrating in CTE programs, which has increased to 90.18%. CTE programs are also vital to the economy and business by closing the skills gap in the STEM jobs that are hardest to fill (ACTE). However, a volume does not currently exist in *New Directions for Community Colleges* that focuses specifically on STEM education, preparation, and career exploration as they relate to the community college environment. More specifically, little information is provided across community college research that examines the specific role of community colleges and career and technical education and STEM. With the current economic push to prepare individuals for careers in STEM, and the essential task of community colleges in preparing individuals for these careers, focusing on exemplary CTE programs and programs that concentrate on educating and preparing individuals for careers in STEM is necessary. The editors and contributors for this *New Directions for Community Colleges* volume respond to the needs of the STEM workforce by highlighting CTE-STEM programs and the exemplary practices within them.

    This volume of *New Directions for Community Colleges* examines the literature on STEM education, preparation, and career exploration.

Additionally, attention is given to the role of CTE in preparing individuals for the STEM workforce. Exemplary practices related to STEM preparation are examined and highlighted. Finally, the issue authors present implications for practice and policy as they relate to CTE. CTE, in this context, is also referred to as vocational education and/or workforce development. The topics in this volume are covered over three sections: (1) incorporating experiential learning activities for students in CTE-STEM programs, (2) providing avenues and effective strategies for closing the skills gap for students in CTE-STEM through funding and evaluation and assessment activities, and (3) highlighting the experiences of women in CTE-STEM related programs. Chapter 8 concludes the volume with implications for policy and practice.

Incorporating Experiential Learning Activities for Students in CTE Programs

The opening chapter provides a landscape of community college pathways to STEM. In this chapter Michelle Van Noy and Matthew Zeidenberg provide a national picture for understanding the characteristics of students in STEM, the varied definitions of STEM, the different types of STEM programs—both academic and workforce oriented—within the community college environment, and STEM pathways. The authors conclude by providing innovative approaches to curriculum, pedagogy, and course development and delivery to ensure the success of all students in STEM related areas.

The second chapter focuses on the essential nature of partnerships in improving student success in STEM, with a particular focus on manufacturing programs at a large urban 2-year technical college. In this chapter, Xueli Wang, Yan Wang, and Amy Prevost explore the experiences of students in contextualized math course offerings to understand how the researcher–practitioner partnership, which is the combination of instructional strategies and concrete application in a specific context, affected student's self-efficacy about themselves and their abilities. The authors further discuss the importance of integrating research and innovation to transfer remedial math in an effort to increase overall student success.

In Chapter 3, by Edgar Troudt, Stuart Schulman, and Christoph Winkler, a virtual enterprise is explored as a means for providing career and technical education. Although similar to Wang, Wang, and Prevost who highlight the role of partnerships in student success, Troudt, Schulman, and Winkler draw attention to simulation as a vehicle for career and technical education. Operated by the City University of New York's Institute for Virtual Enterprise, entrepreneurial simulations bridge practice and competency models that allow students the opportunity to build the necessary skills sets required by the new STEM economy. A full description of the innovative simulation system and a discussion on ways to successfully

NEW DIRECTIONS FOR COMMUNITY COLLEGES • DOI: 10.1002/cc

implement the system to fill a gap in STEM education and its long-term sustainability are provided.

Providing Avenues and Effective Strategies for Closing the Skills Gap for Students in CTE Through Funding and Evaluation and Assessment Activities

In Chapter 4, Kimberly Lowry and Tricia Thomas-Anderson add another dimension to increasing student success by highlighting the idea of closing the skills gap through funding innovations for career and technical education programs. The authors discuss the funding gap among 2-year and 4-year institutions and highlight promising funding avenues, such as the American Graduation Initiative, to improve community college student success, performance, and ultimately graduation rates. Increasing funding opportunities for community college CTE programs allows community colleges to do what they do best—"educate large numbers of less prepared students to their own levels of success," (The Century Foundation Task Force on Preventing Community Colleges from Becoming Separate and Unequal, 2013, p.6)and provide students with the skills necessary to positively affect our nation's economic workforce.

The fifth chapter takes a more outcomes-based approach and discusses the importance of program evaluation and the evaluation of equity gaps in CTE and STEM pathways and programs for underserved student populations. The author discusses federal CTE legislation and how evaluation is considered and used for program review and improvement. Specific to this chapter, Debra Bragg discusses an approach to program improvement called Pathways to Results that began in Illinois. Bragg notes the guiding principles for the evaluation of the approach, critical processes for improving the pathways and programs, and the processes and steps used in Pathways to Results. The author concludes by highlighting lessons for practitioners regarding program evaluation.

Highlighting the Experiences of Women in CTE-Related Programs

Chapter 6 discusses gender inequities in CTE classrooms. In this chapter, Jamie Lester, Brice Struthers, and Aoi Yamanaka highlight microaggression and its role in the experiences and progression of women in CTE programs. More specifically, the chapter highlights the literature related to classroom climates, faculty–student interaction, and the overall landscape of gender-related nuances in CTE courses. Using an ethnographic case study, the authors explore the experiences of female students at a mid-Atlantic community college in typically male-dominated career and technical education courses. The authors discuss the development of the research study and the study's findings and implications for practice as they relate to pedagogy and professional development.

In Chapter 7, Chen, Kemis, and de la Mora take a focused approach in exploring the experiences of women in information technology (IT) in Iowa. In this chapter, the authors highlight the challenges of recruiting and retaining women in IT. The authors begin by discussing the gender imbalance and the social and economic needs related to gender equity and equality. A study conducted by the authors with IT program coordinators, faculty members, and academic counselors at three Iowa community colleges with well-established IT programs revealed factors that encourage women to consider IT as a career choice, exemplary practices related to recruiting and retaining women in IT, as well as challenges of recruiting and retaining women in IT. The authors conclude with recommendations for community college professions as well as researchers and evaluators.

In considering the role of CTE programs in preparing a competent STEM workforce, this book sheds light on the importance of applied and hands-on learning, avenues and effective strategies for closing the skills gap, and the experiences of women and the role of gender in CTE programs. Dimitra Smith concludes the volume (Chapter 8) with a summary of the aforementioned chapters, implications for policy and practice, and lessons for the future of CTE programs and STEM education.

Dimitra Jackson Smith
Soko Starobin
Editors

References

Lacey, T. A., & Wright, B. (2009). Employment outlook: 2008-18-occupational employment projections to 2018. *Monthly Lab. Rev.*, *132*, 82.

Reeve, E. M. (2013). Implementing Science, Technology, Mathematics, and Engineering (STEM) Education in Thailand and in ASEAN.

STEMconnector® (2012). Where are the STEM students? National Report, Washington. Retrieved September 6, 2012 from http://www.stemconnector.org/sites/default/files/store/STEM-Students-STEM-Jobs-Executive-Summary.pdf.

The Century Foundation Task Force on Preventing Community Colleges from Becoming Separate and Unequal (2013). *Bridging the Higher Education Divide: Strengthening Community Colleges and Restoring the American Dream* (Washington, DC: The Century Foundation).

DIMITRA JACKSON SMITH *is a tenured associate professor in the Department of Educational Psychology and Leadership (Higher Education Program) at Texas Tech University in Lubbock, Texas.*

SOKO STAROBIN *is an education consultant/evaluator.*

1

This chapter describes community college STEM programs, including transfer-oriented science and engineering (S&E) programs and workforce-oriented technician programs, and the characteristics and educational pathways of the students who enroll in these programs.

Community College Pathways to the STEM Workforce: What Are They, Who Follows Them, and How?

Michelle Van Noy, Matthew Zeidenberg

Community colleges have a potentially significant and distinctive role in preparing the science, technology, engineering, and mathematics (STEM) workforce. With their open-access mission, affordable tuition, and locations in almost every community, they enroll nearly half of the nation's undergraduate students, including high numbers of low-income and first-generation college students, many seeking to transfer to 4-year schools (American Association of Community Colleges, 2014). Further, their mission of serving local workforce needs motivates community colleges to offer a wide array of subbaccalaureate programs with immediate relevance to employment. As a result, community colleges provide opportunities to prepare for the STEM workforce in a range of program areas to a diverse group of students.

Increasingly community colleges have been recognized for their role in STEM education. For example, a recent National Research Council report, *Community Colleges in the Evolving STEM Education Landscape*, highlighted the important role of community colleges in STEM education as well as the challenges that community college STEM programs face (Olson & Labov, 2012). Although community colleges are not new to STEM education—for instance, the National Science Foundation's Advanced Technological Education program has been actively promoting their role for over 20 years—this recent attention heightens interest in better understanding the contributions of community colleges to STEM education.

NEW DIRECTIONS FOR COMMUNITY COLLEGES, no. 178, Summer 2017 © 2017 Wiley Periodicals, Inc.
Published online in Wiley Online Library (wileyonlinelibrary.com) • DOI: 10.1002/cc.20249

Existing research on community college STEM education has highlighted the role of community colleges in STEM education in several specific areas. Many studies have examined the unique role of community college in broadening participation among female and minority populations (e.g., Jackson & Laanan, 2011; Reyes, 2011; Starobin & Laanan, 2008; Wang, 2013). Research on community college STEM students has focused on specific types of STEM programs such as manufacturing (e.g., Wang, Chan, Phelps, & Washbon, 2012) or information technology (e.g., Van Noy & Weiss, 2011). Other research has provided valuable contributions to understanding the policies and practices related to implementing community college STEM programs (e.g., Hull, 2011).

Looking at students in STEM programs in community colleges, scholars have argued that community colleges can make a unique contribution by providing access to STEM education for underrepresented groups and responding to local labor market needs (Hagedorn & Purnamasari, 2012). Other analyses have begun to provide information on the characteristics and experiences of 2-year college students enrolled in STEM programs nationally (e.g., Chen, 2009, 2013).

To build on this research, this chapter seeks to broadly describe the role of community colleges in STEM education and in workforce preparation nationally. To do this, we examine the following questions: What STEM programs do community college students enroll in and what are the characteristics of these students? and What are the pathways and outcomes of community college STEM students?

A National Picture of Students in STEM Programs

To paint a national picture of students in STEM programs in community colleges, we use the National Center for Education Statistics' (NCES) Beginning Postsecondary Students (BPS) 2004/09 survey. The survey respondents are a nationally representative cohort of students enrolled in postsecondary education for the first time in 2003–2004 in credit-bearing programs.[1,2] Students were surveyed once at the end of their first academic year in 2003–2004, a second time in 2005–2006, and a final time in 2008–2009, 6 years after their initial enrollment. The BPS 04/09 dataset includes a total of 16,684 students. In addition to student interviews, the BPS includes transcript data from all institutions that each student attended from the 2003–2004 to 2008–2009 academic years. We focus this analysis on students who were initially enrolled in a community college in the 2003–2004 academic year—a total of 5,489 students. For comparison, when appropriate, we analyze students who initially enrolled in a 4-year public or private non-for-profit institutions—a total of 8,327 students.

In defining STEM, we include the programs most commonly taken as such: biology, math, engineering, physical sciences, computer and information systems, engineering technicians, science technologies and technicians, and agriculture. These programs have been typically included in definitions of STEM in prior NCES studies using these data (Chen, 2009, 2013). We organize these programs that are commonly defined as STEM into two main categories, as further discussed later.

Limitations of This Study

This study has one main limitation: it is descriptive in nature. So, for instance, we do not develop any models of access and progression in STEM in community colleges. We also do not attempt to control for differences in background, such as family income or academic preparation, which may partially account for the observed raw differences between groups, such as between men and women or between whites and African Americans. Instead, we are painting the existing landscape without attempting to describe the factors that produced it.

In addition, we are limited in the size of the dataset that we are using. This does not, for instance, allow us to say anything about individual states or smaller regions. The dataset is not representative of these entities; it is representative only of the nation.

Identifying STEM Students

We identify whether a student is in a STEM program using two BPS data items: student interviews and student transcripts. First, measures of students' majors for each year of the survey were collected from student interviews and supplemented with institutional information when not available from the interviews. In each of the three BPS interviews, students were asked if they had declared a major (which in a community college may be their program of study). Those with a declared major were asked about their major or field of study. If a student did not report a major, the survey used information on the student's major as reported by their institution. Using these measures, we identify those students enrolled in STEM programs throughout their enrollment in college over the years of the survey. These data are primarily based on self-reports and reflect students' intentions to major in a program. Second, transcript data were collected after the 6-year survey follow-up. These data reflect the majors in which students officially completed a credential, though they do not reflect changes in students' majors over time. We use student transcript data to identify the students' majors upon completion.

Types of STEM Programs

Community colleges offer numerous STEM programs that prepare students for various occupational goals. These programs fall into two main categories: science and engineering (S&E) programs and technician programs.

Table 1.1   Community College Enrollments by Program, Ever Enrolled
in the 6 Years After College Entry Among First-Time Students Who
Began College in 2003–2004

	Number of Students	Percentage of Students
Science and Engineering Programs		
Biological and Biomedical Sciences	42,152	2.6
Engineering	34,530	2.1
Physical Sciences	23,776	1.4
Mathematics and Statistics	9,134	0.6
Total Science and Engineering	109,592	6.6
Technician Programs		
Engineering Technologies	43,631	2.6
Computer and Information Sciences	101,264	6.1
Science Technologies/Technicians	5,357	0.3
Agriculture	17,577	1.1
Total Technician	167,829	10.2

Source: BPS 04/09

The key distinction between these types of programs is whether they require more education (that is, completion of a 4-year degree) to lead to a STEM career or prepare students to enter a STEM career immediately upon completion. S&E programs prepare students for occupations that typically require a bachelor's degree or greater for entry. Through these programs, community colleges provide the opportunity for students to complete the first 2 years of college, attain an associate degree in arts or science (AA or AS), and then transfer to a 4-year institution (Boggs, 2010). These programs include biology, engineering, physical sciences, and mathematics. They comprise nearly 7% of total community college enrollments (Table 1.1).

Technician programs, on the other hand, prepare students for occupations that typically can be entered with a subbaccalaureate credential—such as an associate degree in applied science (AAS) or other credentials including certificates or diplomas. These programs include engineering technologies, computer and information sciences, science technologies, and agriculture. They comprise over 10% of total community college enrollments (Table 1.1). These programs have an important role in workforce development, because nearly one quarter of the STEM workforce is composed of workers with a subbaccalaureate education (Langdon, McKittrick, Khan, & Doms, 2011). Technician programs generally lead to educational credentials, such as certificates, diplomas, or associate degrees and provide work-relevant knowledge and skills. Students who begin in technician programs may also continue on to attain a bachelor's degree, as many such programs do have articulated pathways to 4-year degrees and some jobs for technicians do prioritize bachelor's degree holders (Makela, Rudd, Bennett, & Bragg, 2012). Nationally, community colleges have a long history of

NEW DIRECTIONS FOR COMMUNITY COLLEGES • DOI: 10.1002/cc

Table 1.2   Community College Student Credential Goals, By Program

	All STEM	S&E	Technician	Non-STEM
Credential Goal (%)				
Bachelor's	68	81	60	62
Associate or Certificate	28	15	35	33
None	5	4	5	5

Source: BPS 04/09

providing technician education in a range of fields, some of which are not offered by 4-year institutions (Hull, 2011).

Community college students' credential goals reflect the different program orientations across S&E and technician programs. Among community college technician students, 35% reported that their goal was to obtain an associate degree or certificate, compared with only 15% of community college S&E students (see Table 1.2). Similarly, whereas 60% of technician students reported that they ultimately sought a bachelor's degree, 80% of S&E students sought bachelor's degrees. Although some technician programs at community colleges are transfer oriented, such as in computer and information science, these programs provide students with skills that can lead to immediate employment while they pursue further education.

STEM Student Characteristics

Community college STEM students who were in S&E and technician programs share several key characteristics that make them distinctively unique from the 4-year STEM student population. Community college STEM students were, on average, older and more likely to be first-generation college students than were the 4-year STEM students (see Table 1.3). Although nearly all 4-year students were in the traditional college age range of 18–22 upon enrollment in college, less than three quarters of the first-time community college students were in this age range upon enrollment.[3] A higher proportion of community college STEM students were first-generation college students than were 4-year STEM students (68% versus 38%). In addition, community college STEM students were more likely to be working while enrolled than were 4-year students (76% versus 55%), and of those students who did work, community college STEM students were more likely to work more hours (30 hours per week versus 19 hours). Generally, all of these things—greater age, first-generation status, and working while enrolled—are considered challenges for students in terms of successful completion of college (Goldrick-Rab, 2010). Another major challenge facing community college STEM students is the high proportion who were underprepared and required developmental education compared to 4-year STEM students (69% versus 31%). These differences are reflective of the differences between community college and 4-year students, more broadly.

Table 1.3 STEM Student Characteristics

	Community College Students				Four-Year Students	
Student characteristics	All STEM	S&E	Technician	Non-STEM	STEM	Non-STEM
Race/ethnicity (%)						
White	65	61	68	60	67	71
Black or African American	11	8	13	15	9	10
Hispanic/Latino	14	15	12	16	9	10
Asian American	6	11	4	4	9	5
All other	4	5	4	5	5	5
Female (%)	30	40	24	62	37	62
Pell Grant recipients (%)	26	24	27	29	26	28
First-generation college student (%)	68	62	72	73	38	46
Disabled (%)	12	10	14	11	7	8
Age (%)						
18–22	72	83	66	65	95	92
22–40	23	16	27	26	4	6
40+	5	1	8	8	0	2
Average age upon enrollment	22	20	23	24	19	20
Dependent children (%)	17	12	19	26	2	5
Veteran (%)	4	1	6	3	1	0
Working while enrolled (%)	76	78	74	78	55	62
Average hours worked (among those working)	30	28	30	30	19	21
Developmental education in first year (%)						
Any	69	64	72	68	31	39
Math	59	56	61	59	23	31
English	14	13	15	18	6	8
Reading	15	15	16	19	4	6

Source: BPS 04/09

Community college STEM programs—both S&E and technician—share many of the same fundamental challenges that community colleges face more broadly. On average, community college STEM students are similar to community college students at large on each of the following attributes: age, first-generation college student status, work status while enrolled, and developmental education requirements. Apart from these characteristics, the major difference between community college STEM students and community college students at large is the low proportion of women enrolled in community college STEM programs (30% versus 62%)—a similar phenomenon is found in 4-year colleges as well.

Though they had many characteristics in common, community college S&E and technician students were distinct from each other in important ways that related to the challenges that they faced. Overall S&E students were somewhat more similar to 4-year STEM students, whereas technician students were somewhat more similar to the community college non-STEM population, in the sense that the former group tended to be younger, were less likely to be first generation, and are better prepared academically, which are characteristics of 4-year students as compared with community college students. Although both S&E and technician students were older than 4-year students, S&E programs tended to enroll more young, traditional college-age students than did the technician programs; 83% of S&E students were between 18 and 22 compared with 66% of technician students. Furthermore, although both S&E and technician programs provide access for first-generation college students, technician programs enrolled a greater proportion of first-generation students than did S&E programs (72% versus 62%). S&E students are also less likely to take developmental education than were technician students (64% versus 72%).

S&E and technician programs differed in their enrollment by race/ethnicity and gender. S&E programs enrolled relatively high proportions of Latino and Asian American students. Latinos comprised a larger proportion of community college STEM enrollments, particularly in S&E programs, than of 4-year STEM enrollments (14% in community college STEM overall and 15% in community college S&E programs versus 9% in 4-year STEM programs). Asian American students constituted a greater proportion of community college enrollments in S&E programs (11%) than they did in technician (4%) or non-STEM programs (4%); they had equally high enrollments at 4-year colleges (9%). On the other hand, African American students at community colleges comprised a lower proportion of S&E programs (8%) than the technician programs (13%) and non-STEM programs (15%). Wang's (2013) analysis of the representation of racial and ethnic minorities in STEM education in community colleges using the BPS data finds similar results; however, it is restricted to students with a STEM major in their first year of enrollment. Technician programs disproportionately enrolled students who were White and male. White students enrolled at higher rates in technician programs (68%) than S&E (61%) and non-STEM programs (60%). Women enrolled at lower rates in technician programs (24%) relative to S&E (40%) and non-STEM programs (62%).

STEM Student Pathways

Given the variety of STEM programs and the distinct characteristics of students who enroll in them, we next examined students' enrollment patterns across these programs. Enrollment patterns include intensity of enrollment (full time and part time), continuous enrollment versus breaks in time between terms of enrollment, and enrollment at multiple institutions. Community college students' enrollment patterns are important because enrollment continuity is positively associated with completion rates and enrollment intensity is positively associated with transfer rates (Crosta, 2014). Community college students' movement between multiple institutions, a pattern sometimes termed *swirling*, is associated with lower completion rates (Goldrick-Rab, 2006).

Full-time continuous enrollment was not the norm among community college STEM students as it was among 4-year STEM students. Only one third of both S&E and technician students attended college full time for the duration of their enrollment, compared with two thirds of 4-year STEM students (see Table 1.4). In addition, over half of community college STEM students—both S&E and technician—had at least one break of 4 months or more (that is, longer than a summer) in their enrollment; less than one third of 4-year STEM students have a similar break in enrollment. Interestingly, the proportion of students swirling among multiple institutions (more than the two involved in a traditional transfer) is similar across groups—about one quarter of community college STEM students, 4-year STEM students, as well as community college non-STEM students attend multiple institutions in the 6-year period after their initial college enrollment. These unstable enrollment patterns have major implications for how students progress along STEM pathways, their time to completion, and their ultimate ability to complete, given that articulation between institutions often has complications. Job and family responsibilities can interfere with the ability to go to school continuously and full time.

Although the enrollment patterns of S&E and technician students were similar, some differences among these groups highlight the specific characteristics and goals of their students. Technician students were more likely to attend part time exclusively than were S&E students (15% versus 8%) and were more likely to have multiple stop-outs (15% versus 8%). These more unstable enrollment patterns likely reflect the somewhat more nontraditional population of older students in the technician program. In keeping with their goal of attaining a subbaccalaureate credential, technician students were more likely to concentrate their attendance at only one institution—the community college—than were the S&E students (59% versus 33%). On the other hand, S&E students were more likely to follow

Table 1.4 Enrollment Patterns Among Community College STEM Students, by Subfield

	Community College Students				Four-Year Students	
	All STEM	S&E	Technician	Non-STEM	STEM	Non-STEM
Average enrollment intensity (%)						
Always full time	33	36	32	27	68	65
Always part time	13	8	15	22	1	2
Mixed part time & full time	53	55	53	51	31	33
Constancy of attendance/number of stop-outs (%)						
0	47	49	46	50	71	72
1	41	43	39	35	22	21
2+	12	8	15	15	7	7
Institutional attendance (%)						
Attend only one institution	49	33	59	62	75	74
Traditional transfer	25	41	16	19	NA	NA
Attend multiple institutions, swirling	26	26	25	19	25	26

Source: BPS 04/09

Table 1.5   Outcomes Among Community College STEM Students
6 Years After Enrollment

Outcome	All	S&E	Technician
Attained STEM credential within 6 years (%)			
Any credential	19	21	20
Bachelor's	10	16	7
Associate or certificate	9	5	13
Still enrolled in STEM 6 years after initial enrollment (%)			
At any institution	16	19	14
At community college	7	6	8
At 4-year college	8	13	6
Transferred to 4-year college in STEM at time in 6 years (%)	25	37	19
Stayed in STEM—attained credential or still enrolled	30	33	30
Moved to non-STEM—attained credential or still enrolled	33	39	29
Dropped out without credential	37	27	41

Source: BPS 04/09
Note: Students may be included in more than one category because students may obtain multiple outcomes like attaining a credential and transferring.

a traditional transfer pathway than the technician students—that is, they initially enrolled at the community college and then transferred to a 4-year college (41% versus 16%). The differences in enrollment patterns between S&E and technician students reflect their differences in characteristics and goals.

Although credential completion rates are relatively low for STEM students, many students were still enrolled in STEM by the end of the 6-year period (see Table 1.5). Six years after their initial STEM enrollment, 21% of S&E students and 20% of technician students had attained any STEM credential. As would be expected given their goals, technician students were more likely to attain an associate degree or certificate than S&E students (13% versus 5%), and S&E students were more likely to attain a bachelor's degree than technician students (16% versus 7%). In addition to completion, 19% of S&E students and 14% of technician students were still enrolled in a STEM program at some institution. S&E students were more likely to still be enrolled at a 4-year college 6 years after enrollment than were technician students (13% versus 6%). This may indicate that many students pursuing an S&E pathway need more than 6 years to complete a bachelor's degree. Likewise, technician students with unstable enrollment patterns may also require more time to attain a credential.

To put these outcomes in context, on the whole community college STEM students have better outcomes than other community college students. Over half of the non-STEM community college students (52%) dropped out after 6 years, compared with 37% of STEM students. These differences may reflect greater motivation among community college STEM students than non-STEM students as opposed to ability; their ability as reflected in developmental education participation was similar. They may also reflect differences in STEM students' experiences in college that may be associated with better retention in college, albeit not necessarily in STEM.

Whether students stay in STEM—by either completing a STEM credential or continuing enrollment in a STEM program—varied by S&E and technician programs. Six years after their initial enrollment, one third of community college students who were initially in STEM remained STEM (Table 1.4). Students who were initially in S&E and technician fields were equally likely to still be in a STEM field 6 years after enrollment. However, the trajectories of those who left STEM were quite different across S&E and technician students. Technician students were more likely to drop out than S&E students (37% versus 27%), whereas S&E students were more likely to switch to a non-STEM field than technician students (39% versus 27%). Technician students may drop out at relatively higher rates because of their more unstable enrollment patterns and because of the possibility that some may obtain employment with skills they have already attained from selected STEM courses (Booth & Bahr, 2013; Washbon, 2013).

Conclusions and Recommendations

The national picture of community college students in STEM and technician programs leads to several conclusions for community college S&E and technician programs. We discuss these conclusions and make recommendations for future research and practice.

To the extent that community college STEM programs seek to provide access and equity to traditionally underrepresented groups, more attention should be given to their enrollment patterns across S&E and technician programs, as well as recruitment and retention of underrepresented groups. Community colleges provide opportunities for STEM education, particularly for Latino and Asian American students, to pursue S&E programs that lead to entrée into 4-year STEM programs. The high proportion of enrollments in technician programs by students who are White and male also raises questions about the opportunities in these programs for students from diverse backgrounds, as these programs can facilitate transitions to well-paying jobs upon completion.

Community college STEM programs may apply innovative approaches from 4-year STEM programs to the specific needs of their students. Although community college STEM students share some similarities with 4-year college students, they have distinct needs and interests. Experiences that serve to engage students in applying their STEM learning but in ways that also serve the typical interests of older students in learning relevant skills for the workforce are particularly needed.

Community college STEM programs face similar challenges with respect to their student population as do non-STEM programs in the community college and thus will benefit from overall community college reform efforts. Reforms that consider how community colleges can better serve older students and make college more affordable will be important. Developmental education reform, particularly in math, is a major priority for community colleges at large and is of particular relevance to community college STEM students.

The lengthy persistence of community college STEM students, particularly S&E students, requires community colleges to employ new strategies and outcome measures. Although low completion rates among community college STEM students are a major concern, their high persistence rates are notable. They take a long time to finish with a good deal of enrollment that is part time or interrupted, but many do persist. This persistence raises questions about what programs can do differently to help students finish sooner.

Adapted and reproduced with permission from the National Academy of Sciences, Courtesy of the National Academies Press, Washington, DC.

Notes

1. BPS does not include students enrolled in noncredit programs, although these programs may play an important role in STEM education (Hagedorn & Purnamasari, 2012).
2. The BPS does not provide information on STEM students who have had some prior postsecondary experience. Therefore, this sample may understate the issues of older and returning students.
3. The BPS includes only first-time students; returning students with prior college education are not included. Thus, the BPS may include a relatively younger student population than actually represented in community college STEM programs.

References

American Association of Community Colleges. (2014). *2014 fact sheet.* Washington, DC: Author. Retrieved from http://www.aacc.nche.edu/AboutCC/Documents/Facts14_Data_R2.pdf

Boggs, G. R. (2010). Growing roles for science education in community colleges. *Science,* 329(5996), 1151–1152.

Booth, K., & Bahr, P. (2013). *The missing piece: Quantifying non-completion pathways to success.* San Francisco, CA: WestEd.

Chen, X. (2009). *Students who study science, technology, engineering, and mathematics (STEM) in postsecondary education.* Washington, DC: National Center for Education Statistics, Institute of Education Sciences, U.S. Department of Education.

Chen, X. (2013). *STEM attrition: College students' paths into and out of STEM fields* (NCES 2014-001). Washington, DC: National Center for Education Statistics, Institute of Education Sciences, U.S. Department of Education.

Crosta, P. (2014). Intensity and attachment: How the chaotic enrollment patterns of community college students relate to educational outcomes. *Community College Review,* 42(2), 1–25.

Goldrick-Rab, S. (2006). Following their every move: How social class shapes postsecondary pathways. *Sociology of Education,* 79(1), 61–79.

Goldrick-Rab, S. (2010). Challenges and opportunities for improving community college student success. *Review of Educational Research,* 80(3), 437–469.

Hagedorn, L., & Purnamasari, S. (2012). A realistic look at STEM and the role of community colleges. *Community College Review, 40*(2), 145–164.

Hull, D. (2011). *Career pathways for STEM technicians.* Waco, TX: Op-TEC.

Jackson, D., & Laanan, F. (2011). The role of community colleges in educating women in science and engineering. In J. G. Gayles (Ed.), *New Directions for Institutional Research: No. 152. Attracting and retaining women in STEM* (pp. 39–49). San Francisco, CA: Jossey-Bass.

Langdon, D., McKittrick, G., Khan, B., & Doms, M. (2011). *STEM: Good jobs now and for the future.* Washington, DC: U.S. Department of Commerce.

Makela, J., Rudd, C., Bennett, S., & Bragg, D. (2012). *Investigating applied baccalaureate degree pathways in technician education.* Urbana-Champaign, IL: Office of Community College Research and Leadership, University of Illinois.

Olson, S., & Labov, J. (2012). *Community colleges in the evolving STEM education landscape: Summary of a summit.* Washington, DC: National Academies Press. Retrieved from http://www.nap.edu/catalog.php?record_id=13399

Reyes, M. (2011). Unique challenges for women of color in STEM transferring from community colleges. *Harvard Educational Review, 81*(2), 241–262.

Starobin, S., & Laanan, F. (2008). Broadening female participation in science, technology, engineering, and mathematics: Experiences at community colleges. In J. Lester (Ed.), *New Directions for Community Colleges: No. 142. Gendered perspectives on community colleges* (pp. 37–46). San Francisco, CA: Jossey-Bass.

Van Noy, M., & Weiss, M. J. (2010). *The role of community college education in the employment of information technology workers in Washington State* (CCRC Working Paper No. 23). New York, NY: Community College Research Center, Teachers College, Columbia University.

Wang, X., Chan, H., Phelps, L. A., & Washbon, J. (2012). *Students in manufacturing and other STEM fields at two-year colleges: An exploration of aspirations and enrollment.* Madison, WI: Wisconsin Center for Education Research at the School of Education, University of Wisconsin-Madison.

Wang, X. (2013). Community colleges and underrepresented racial and ethnic minorities in STEM education: A national picture. In R. T. Palmer & J. L. Wood (Eds.), *Community colleges and STEM: Examining underrepresented racial and ethnic minorities.* New York: Routledge, Taylor & Francis Group.

Washbon, J. (2013). *Jobbing out: A preliminary analysis of student attrition in METTE programs in Wisconsin.* Madison, WI: Wisconsin Center for Education Research at the School of Education, University of Wisconsin-Madison.

MICHELLE VAN NOY *is associate director of the Education and Employment Research Center and assistant research professor of Labor Studies and Employment Relations at the School of Management and Labor Relations at Rutgers, the State University of New Jersey.*

MATTHEW ZEIDENBERG *is a senior scientist at Abt Associates, Bethesda, Maryland.*

NEW DIRECTIONS FOR COMMUNITY COLLEGES • DOI: 10.1002/cc

2

This chapter documents a partnership between university-based researchers and community college instructors and practitioners in their collective pursuit to improve student success in manufacturing programs at a large urban 2-year technical college, presenting an example of a contextualized instructional approach to teaching developmental math, tightly coupled with research activities that inform instructional practices.

A Researcher–Practitioner Partnership on Remedial Math Contextualization in Career and Technical Education Programs

Xueli Wang, Yan Wang, Amy Prevost

In the national discourse on improving student success within career and technical education (CTE) programs, few issues attract as much focus as setting students on the right trajectory toward earning a credential. A roadblock to achieving this goal, however, is the troublesome fact that many CTE-aspiring students arrive at 2-year colleges underprepared in basic skills and struggle to pass remedial sequences, notably in math (Bahr, 2013; Bailey, 2009; Boatman & Long, 2010; Scott-Clayton & Rodriguez, 2012). Thus, improving remedial math outcomes represents a pivotal issue of concern for CTE, especially considering math's strong predictive power for later academic progress and its use in CTE careers (Bahr, 2013).

Along with this shared understanding of the need to improve remedial math is the sore reality that, across the remedial curriculum, math is often imparted in separation from substantive subjects of students' interest (Perin, 2011). Too often, remedial math is structured by a review-and-lecture mode, detached from any context beyond the classroom (Grubb, 2010). This decontextualized approach is problematic for CTE students, as it isolates them from the applicability of math in occupational fields and is likely to result in low completion rates (Grubb & Associates, 1999).

It then becomes obvious that, to reinvent remedial math, a contextualized approach to instruction offers a promising lens. Contextualization is defined as "a diverse family of instructional strategies designed to more

NEW DIRECTIONS FOR COMMUNITY COLLEGES, no. 178, Summer 2017 © 2017 Wiley Periodicals, Inc.
Published online in Wiley Online Library (wileyonlinelibrary.com) • DOI: 10.1002/cc.20250

23

seamlessly link the learning of foundational skills and academic or occupational content by focusing teaching and learning squarely on concrete applications in a specific context that is of interest to the student" (Mazzeo, 2008, p. 3). Within this broad definition, contextualization takes a number of instructional formats, including but not limited to, integration of basic skills with subject matter courses, contextualizing a basic skills course with a companion course (such as hands-on workshops), or teaching basic skills with direct reference to real-life examples.

Although the research literature has both problematized remedial math instruction in CTE and pinpointed the vast potential of contextualization to solve this problem (e.g., Perin, 2011), in reality, educational practices are not always well informed by research evidence, and implementation of education innovations is often disconnected from data-driven decisions. Thus, there is a pressing need to bring together the communities of researchers and practitioners concerned about the same issues, in order to make concerted efforts, driven and informed by empirical evidence, to enhance CTE student success. In this chapter, we describe how university-based researchers worked with CTE program leaders, instructors, and institutional researchers at a 2-year college to contextualize remedial math within manufacturing programs. Our discussion of and reflections upon this researcher–practitioner partnership, relatively rare in CTE settings, offer several implications and recommendations for reforming remedial math instruction in CTE and for future partnerships that focus on improving CTE student success.

Partnership Background

This partnership materialized as the result of a targeted research project housed within the Wisconsin Center for Education Research at the University of Wisconsin (UW)-Madison, funded by the Advanced Technological Education (ATE) program of the National Science Foundation (NSF, Award No. 1104226). This project focused on improving student success within manufacturing engineering technologist and technician education (METTE) programs at Wisconsin's 2-year colleges. Two-year community and technical colleges play a major role in addressing concerns about shortages of students qualified to work in METTE careers. Thus, our project centered on improving METTE student success by producing evidence that informs institutional policy and practices. One of the features of this work is that it engaged university-based researchers and 2-year college faculty and administrators in working collaboratively toward achieving the common goal of student success. This working group followed the model set forth by the Carnegie Foundation (Bryk, Gomez, & Grunow, 2010), referred to as a Networked Improvement Community (NIC). Within a NIC, individuals in varied roles are intentionally brought together to help create sustainable changes that lead to improved educational outcomes.

New Directions for Community Colleges • DOI: 10.1002/cc

Members of NICs work toward meeting shared, measurable targets and subsequently use what is learned to set new goals. Accordingly, in our partnership, university researchers contribute research tools as well as expertise in using them. Practitioners offer valuable insights into the classroom context and their student body. Following this model, our targeted research project developed four NICs involving researchers at UW-Madison and four technical colleges in Wisconsin to address specific issues surrounding METTE student success at each of these institutions. In this chapter, we showcase one such example at Milwaukee Area Technical College (MATC) where the NIC team built a strategic approach to assessing and addressing math underpreparedness among students aspiring to enter METTE programs and careers.

As a public 2-year comprehensive technical college, MATC's mission centers on providing educational opportunities and services to the diverse metropolitan area where it is located. Playing a central role in workforce development within the state, MATC is an urban, multicampus college with approximately 170 academic programs, serving about 45,000 students each year. Like many other community colleges in the nation that are critical to the completion agenda set forth by the White House (2009) to add an additional 5 million graduates by 2020, MATC signed up for the Completion Challenge with the American Association of Community College in 2010 to identify barriers to students' success. Under this initiative, academic underpreparedness of incoming students was pinpointed as one of the major roadblocks for completing a successful academic career at MATC.

The Need for Contextualizing Math Remediation at MATC

At MATC, access to English and math courses is based on scores from placement tests, namely, Accuplacer Arithmetic, Reading, and Sentence Skills tests. Students with scores in the highest range are placed into postsecondary-level math and/or English courses, along with program specific courses. Students with test scores within the middle and lowest ranges are placed into remedial or developmental math and/or English courses. At the institutional level, there have been ongoing efforts to review these placement cutoff scores to make sure that students are appropriately placed.

Faculty in the welding and machine tooling programs have observed the negative impact of math underpreparedness on their students' success. This observation was supported by analyses of institutional data, suggesting that the highest range cutoff scores needed to be raised to ensure that students are ready for a college-level curriculum. Accordingly, in 2012, MATC raised the math cutoff scores when admitting students into the welding and machine tooling diploma programs. Although this change ensures that admitted students were better prepared in math, one of its consequences was that a number of students who had been previously considered "college ready" were placed into the middle range and needed to take remedial courses. This new policy prompted members involved in our researcher–practitioner partnership to engage in an extensive conversation about how to better address the needs of this new group of students, which served as catalyst for exploring innovations in math learning and teaching for underprepared students at MATC.

Designing the Contextualized Math Courses

Initially, two day-long meetings were held, wherein partners discussed and debated several possible innovation options. Conversations were largely shaped by a collective commitment to college readiness in math among developmental students. Program leaders offered big-picture program and policy contexts and constraints, the institutional researcher provided college-, program-, and course-level data on student enrollment and progress, and faculty members presented realistic insights into student learning and day-to-day instructional practices. During this process, the lead university-based researcher played the role of a moderator and note-taker, facilitated discussions, offered research evidence on math remediation in light of the MATC context, and synthesized recommendations that evolved from the conversations. After the meetings, these summaries were provided to MATC's lead institutional researcher and served as points of departure when engaging with others at MATC. Several options in offering math courses were further explored during these meetings. Ultimately, the team proposed that, instead of restricting the students to remedial math only, this new group of students take postsecondary-level math supported by a concurrent basic skills math course. In addition, they would also take program-specific courses related to welding and machine tooling. Once the general course structure was agreed upon, MATC team members discussed this instructional approach with the lead researcher. A consensus was reached, based on both research and practical experiences, that contextualizing MATC's math offerings for students at the remedial level was the direction that would be taken.

As mentioned earlier, prior research has indicated that contextualization can positively influence outcomes for students in remedial courses, by connecting new knowledge to real-world tasks to ensure deep learning (Perin, 2011). With contextualized approaches, learners become "active agents" in their learning, and are better able to integrate concepts into schema that they have already constructed in past experiences (Ambrose, Davis, & Zeigler, 2013). Although the notion of contextualization was formally brought up by the UW-Madison researcher, its nature was more of a reflection rather than a researcher-driven idea, in response to a thorough discussion of the college's programmatic and instructional contexts, along with practical resource constraints and opportunities.

Indeed, it was the instructors' repeated emphasis on the need to bring a more "hands-on" approach into teaching remedial math that culminated in the decision to introduce contextualization, due to its potential positive impact, and this idea was embraced by all stakeholders at the table. As a result, three specific contextualized offerings were proposed and implemented starting in the fall of 2013: (a) a one-credit math elective designed to contextualize the math concepts taught in a remedial math course; (b) a math class in welding contextualized by an accompanying hands-on workshop, along with a basic skills math course; and (c) a math class in machine tooling contextualized by an accompanying hands-on workshop, along with a basic skills math course. In addition, capitalizing on this momentum of trust and shared commitment, the team also agreed that, in order to inform and guide authentic and robust implementation of the newly contextualized curricula, research assistance from the lead researcher and her team was imperative to both document the innovation process and to gauge its efficacy for later reflection and improvement.

Embedded Research as Ongoing Evaluation of Instruction

In order to both offer timely data to inform the contextualized offerings and generate new empirical knowledge to extend the literature on remedial math instruction, the research team conducted mixed-methods research, collecting both qualitative and quantitative data. The data collection process was in tandem with the math offerings implemented as described previously. To begin with, in fall 2013, we conducted classroom observations and open interviews with two pilot contextualized remedial math classes. After analyzing these data, seeking input from the NIC members, and drawing upon relevant literature (e.g., Ambrose, Davis, & Ziegler, 2013; Bandura, 1977; Perin, 2011), we developed a survey instrument that measured students' learning experiences within contextualized math courses, math self-efficacy beliefs, and assessment of the effectiveness of the adopted contextualized approach. The joint development of the surveys was critical, as collaboration is key to our partnership. Because on a local, on-the-ground level, instructors were interested in directly informing teaching practices, having their input allowed us to consider and include survey questions that informed actionable instructional strategies.

The survey questions allowed us to understand how experiences in contextualized course offerings affected students' beliefs about themselves and their abilities, the strategies that they employed in order to be successful, and how they viewed teaching and learning at MATC. For example, questions designed to understand students' beliefs about themselves and their abilities included scaled items, where students were asked to indicate how much they agreed or disagreed with statements such as "If I work hard to solve a problem, I will find the answer" and "I find it easy to face new challenges in math," along with items related to their readiness to continue with the intended math sequence for their program. Also, importantly, the survey included questions about student experiences in the classroom, such as how often instructors guided students through questions and problems related to math versus only engaging them with lecture materials, and how often students felt that math had been effectively related to their field of study. Of no less value, we also collected data on how student views changed related to how math is used in manufacturing technologies.

We administered paper versions of the survey to students in the three contextualized courses and workshops described previously. In order to protect students' confidentiality, MATC's institutional researcher retrieved the class rosters and assigned each student a study ID to keep student responses anonymous. The institutional researcher then worked with the instructors to schedule a time toward the end of the term to administer the survey within classrooms. After the questionnaires were collected from students who consented to participate, the institutional researcher mailed de-identified, completed questionnaires with study IDs to the researchers at UW-Madison, who then helped with data entry and analysis. As students' academic records became available, they were matched with the survey data using a mapping table between study IDs and student IDs retained by MATC's institutional researcher. Finally, to deepen our understanding of the survey findings, we conducted interviews with students and instructors.

Key Findings from the Researcher–Practitioner Partnership

In the CTE world, a researcher–practitioner partnership is relatively infrequent. Yet, these relationships are extremely valuable and worth promoting: any serious education innovation should be well grounded within a data-driven decision process to both warrant its existence and gauge its efficacy. Equally important, any researcher who is committed to conducting meaningful empirical work on education issues would have their efforts misdirected without a genuine understanding of, and appreciation for, the "messy" realities of our most thorny educational issues, such as remedial math. Given these thoughts, in the ideal CTE world, the researcher and the practitioner work together toward a common goal, maximizing their unique strengths to complement each other's work. Yet, what often happens is a disconnection between researcher and practitioner goals, with practitioners hesitating to embrace research, as they see "academic" approaches often detached from their day-to-day challenges; likewise, researchers are often frustrated by the noises and challenges associated with implementation of the research design. We have to admit that in our partnership, we have experienced such moments on both ends but eventually settled on a pragmatic approach to our partnership, without compromising our shared concern about the problem at hand: improving CTE students' college readiness in math.

What sustained us and our partnership throughout the process was our collective pursuit of innovative approaches that would help crack the remedial barriers for the many underserved students, for whom the CTE programs at MATC may represent their only option for social mobility. This shared commitment enabled us to solve problems and focus on "what works," even if sometimes that meant allowing the research process to be muddy for the researcher, and, for the practitioner, spending hours collecting and discussing data and opening up classroom spaces for observations and interviews.

Contextualization's Influence on Student Learning and Motivation. Though our partnership has been fruitful in many regards, most important, we found that from all three sources of data (i.e., observation, survey, and interview), students seemed to benefit from contextualization to a great extent. From the classroom observations during the pilot stage, we found that when making contextualization their main focus, the welding and machine tooling instructors teaching remedial math purposefully drew linkages between math concepts and their real-world settings, approached mathematical ideas in myriad ways, and encouraged the pursuit of multiple solutions. The close connection between math skills and the CTE subjects (i.e., welding and machine tooling), thus made possible, situated math within future CTE careers to which students aspire. As a result, students became eager to apply math, as they saw its role in the workforce they desire to enter. This increased interest and motivation were evident from both observations and interviews with students involved in the pilot offerings.

Similarly, the survey data more systematically revealed positive findings. Across the board, students reported that the remedial math courses were contextualized to a great extent. For example, about two thirds of the students reported that math problems they worked on in the classroom were often related to their career field, and over 90% of the students believed that math concepts were connected to what they already knew. Almost two thirds of the students were often engaged in group discussions and problem solving, and nearly two thirds of the students reported that their instructor found multiple ways to explain a math concept.

In order to reconstruct the complex picture of findings that surfaced from the survey data, we also conducted interviews with students and instructors involved in the spring 2014 offerings. As a whole, data collected through our observations, surveys, and interviews unfolded a larger, incremental process by which contextualization can help transform CTE students' learning and motivation. As summarized in our research report (Wang, Sun, & Wickersham, in press):

> When math becomes real and accessible, students overcome their initial fear of math that often results from a perceived mismatch between math problems at hand and their math abilities. As contextualization helps tame that fear, by shedding realistic light onto math problems where application of new and prior math skills is tangible, students start to understand math's application.

With true understanding comes appreciation for math's utility, especially in light of the careers students aspire to obtain. It is at this juncture of being able to appreciate math that efficacy in math is being cultivated, which then translates into an overall sense of belief in the self that transcends math, or any specific subject, for that matter . . .

In this sense, our partnership has produced new empirical knowledge on contextualization's positive influence on remedial math students in CTE programs. But considering the nature of an authentic researcher–practitioner partnership, this represents only one of several important benefits and takeaways. In addition to the research evidence, we have also uncovered, through constant reflection and trial and error, several insights into how to better serve underprepared students at 2-year colleges using institutional data, how to sustain promising CTE innovations, especially when such innovations originate from short-term external funding, and finally, how to establish and honor a researcher–practitioner partnership such as ours. In the following, we share these perspectives, in anticipation of using them to inspire a stronger, longer term dialogue on building partnerships between communities of scholars and practitioners collectively invested in the success of CTE programs and students.

Using Institutional Data to Better Serve Underprepared Students. For MATC, this partnership provided robust empirical data to support an education innovation. In addition, it has also brought about a change in the mindset of leaders and practitioners, who have become willing to evaluate new efforts along the way and initiate new strategies as necessary. This transformation is especially pivotal, as MATC has been balancing its open-access mission and the effort of making sure that students are college ready, honoring its long tradition of serving the needs of its diverse student body. Throughout this partnership, all stakeholders involved were committed to improving the learning opportunities for those behind in math, as it is widely known that math is a critical predictor for success.

As the MATC institutional research office is officially charged to evaluate the impact of new initiatives on student success, it became a critical liaison in helping to shape a data-informed culture at MATC. Through presenting ongoing research as a result of this partnership to a wide range of audiences including college leaders, instructional deans, and faculty, MATC's institutional research demonstrated the importance of using data to identify barriers to student success and to facilitate discussions of promising interventions to remove those barriers. In addition, survey and interview data have inspired MATC faculty and administrators to start asking questions about how to gather evidence to document other initiatives' efficacy, how to use other research to evaluate new initiatives, and to make sure that the resources are well allocated and used. This incremental process of institutional change epitomizes what Bailey and Alfonso (2005) lauded when assessing program effectiveness at community colleges, with faculty and administrators fully engaged and institutional research playing a prominent role.

Challenges to Sustaining Improvement Efforts.   One major concern emerging toward the end of this project was how to sustain and institutionalize these innovations, especially given the relatively short-term, external funding available to implement them. Funds from this project have contributed variously to staff and administrator time for attending NIC meetings and data retreats, instructor time devoted to developing and implementing the contextualized course offerings and workshops, and administration of surveys and assessments of students, among other things.

Research has shown that programs that are funded with short-term external sources are most successfully sustained when their goals are tied to wider initiatives (Blumenfeld, Sadrozinski, & Nerad, 2007). In our case, this means tying these goals to initiatives within MATC, as well as to those within the Wisconsin Technical College System (WTCS) as a whole. Engaging a team with crosscutting roles and responsibilities was one way we helped ensure that the initiatives undertaken as part of this project would be sustained. Throughout the project, this team has been able to develop and maintain a partnership related to this work that was mutually beneficial, another hallmark of sustainability.

Though at the outset Networked Improvement Communities may seem like a drain on resources, the hope was that this way of working becomes the new norm and allows for more systemic solutions to complex problems. However, institutionalizing change is a slow process. As Bailey and Alfonso (2005) put it, "research is an investment; its payoff emerges only over time (p. 3)." Change agents must advocate for new processes and procedures to be adopted. This can occur only if efforts are valued and rewarded. Typically, we have seen a competitive, rather than collaborative, approach to innovation within education. Therefore, in order for these changes to take root, organizations need to find ways to support and recognize collaboration as important to student success. In the case of MATC, we have been able to garner support from administrators, faculty, staff, and institutional researchers, who are all on the same page with regard to their commitment to offering and improving contextualized math courses as a cornerstone to student success in METTE programs. Additional contextualized courses continue to be planned and launched, and administrators and institutional researchers are working to become trained in ways that will allow them to continue to evaluate the use of contextualized courses in improving remedial student success.

Putting It All Together: Promoting a Researcher–Practitioner Partnership to Improve CTE Student Outcomes

Our major takeaway from the work described in this chapter is the critical importance of cultivating an authentic researcher–practitioner partnership, which revolves around three major roles: **the researcher, the practitioner, and the data**, with a **shared commitment to student learning and success** as the partnership's underpinning. In this partnership, researchers engage with practitioners and then together explore existing data and collect new data to improve student learning and success. Next, we offer a few recommendations for others wishing to foster a similar partnership in their CTE work.

- First, when working together, researchers and practitioners must honor and offer complementary expertise to one another, in order to serve as catalysts for change. Through this approach, they will be able to collectively drive the use of the partnership that allows research to inform practice.
- Second, such a partnership must center on creating and using high-quality data to inform the direction of research and practice. For example, at MATC, this information continues to shape the contextualized math offerings and is being extended to other areas. For others who wish to engage in similar work, we recommend using equally rich data sources to understand what constitutes educationally beneficial learning activities for their students.
- Third, practitioners and instructors can use their individual expertise to provide CTE students with appropriate supports like advising or specialized course offerings surrounding factors found to be important for academic success and personal well-being. These initiatives can help students find the best fit for their college experience and future career.
- Finally, others aiming to follow a partnership like this should plan to dedicate a lot of time to developing a trusting partnership through engaging in dialogue between each of the key stakeholders involved in the efforts to improve CTE student outcomes. Some activities that might increase success include hosting regular check-ins and honoring the commitments already in place for each stakeholder. This is especially true in the case of practitioners, who are typically not engaged with conducting research and using data in an explicit way. It helps to consider that institutional practices take a long time to change. In our case, we dedicated over 3 years to the process of building the partnership.

As concluding remarks, we reiterate the pivotal role of collecting and using high-quality data in motivating and sustaining our partnership. Team members who engage with one another in this process have to be committed to trying new strategies and letting the data "show them the way." In all, it is our hope that our experiences and recommendations in regard to cultivating a strong researcher-practitioner partnership toward CTE student learning and success can inspire others to engage in similar work.

New Directions for Community Colleges • DOI: 10.1002/cc

References

Ambrose, V. K., Davis, C. A., & Ziegler, M. F. (2013). From research to practice: A framework for contextualizing teaching and learning. *Journal of College Reading and Learning, 44*(1), 35–50.

Bahr, P. R. (2013). The aftermath of remedial math: Investigating the low rate of certificate completion among remedial math students. *Research in Higher Education, 54,* 171–200.

Bailey, T. (2009). Challenge and opportunity: Rethinking the role and function of developmental education in community college. In A. C. Bueschel & A. Venezia (Eds.), *New Directions for Community Colleges: No. 145. Policies and practices to improve student preparation and success* (pp. 11–30). San Francisco, CA: Jossey-Bass. doi:10.1002/cc.352

Bailey, T., & Alfonso, M.(2005). *Paths to persistence: An analysis of research on program effectiveness at community colleges.* New Agenda Series. Indianapolis: Lumina Foundation for Education.

Bandura, A. (1977). Self-efficacy: Toward a unifying theory of behavioral change. *Psychological Review, 84,* 191–215.

Blumenfeld, T., Sadrozinski, R., & Nerad, M. (2007). *Best practices for IGERT sustainability.* Seattle, WA: University of Washington, Center for Innovation and Research in Graduate Education. Retrieved from http://www.education.uw.edu/cirge/best-practices-for-igert-sustainability/

Boatman, A., & Long, B. T. (2010). *Does remediation work for all students? How the effects of postsecondary remedial and developmental courses vary by level of academic preparation* (NCPR Working Paper). New York, NY: National Center for Postsecondary Research. Retrieved from http://files.eric.ed.gov/fulltext/ED512610.pdf

Bryk, A. S., Gomez, L. M., & Grunow, L. (2010). *Getting ideas into action: Building Networked Improvement Communities in education.* Stanford, CA: Carnegie Foundation for the Advancement of Teaching. Retrieved from https://www.carnegiefoundation.org/wp-content/uploads/2014/09/bryk-gomez_building-nics-education.pdf

Grubb, W. N. (2010, September). *The quandaries of basic skills in community colleges: Views from the classroom* (NCPR Working Paper). New York, NY: National Center for Postsecondary Research.

Grubb, W. N., & Associates. (1999). *Honored but invisible: An inside look at teaching in community colleges.* New York, NY: Routledge.

Mazzeo, C. (2008). *Supporting student success at California community colleges: A white paper.* Oakland, CA: Career Ladders Project for California Community Colleges.

Perin, D. (2011). *Facilitating student learning through contextualization* (CCRC Working Paper No. 29). New York, NY: Community College Research Center, Teachers College, Columbia University.

Scott-Clayton, J., & Rodriguez, O. (2012). *Development, discouragement, or diversion? New evidence on the effects of college remediation* (NBER Working Paper No. 18328). Cambridge, MA: National Bureau of Economic Research.

Wang, X., Sun, N., & Wickersham, K. (in press). Turning math remediation into "homeroom": Contextualization as a motivational environment for remedial math students at community colleges. *Review of Higher Education.*

White House. (2009). *Education: Knowledge and skills for the jobs of the future. Support for higher education.* https://obamawhitehouse.archives.gov/issues/education/higher-education

DR. XUELI WANG is an associate professor in the Department of Educational Leadership and Policy Analysis at UW-Madison.

DR. YAN WANG is director of institutional research at Milwaukee Area Technical College.

DR. AMY PREVOST is an assistant researcher at the Wisconsin Center for Education Research.

NEW DIRECTIONS FOR COMMUNITY COLLEGES • DOI: 10.1002/cc

3

This paper explores the model of a pedagogical system for business and entrepreneurship education and discusses the effects of its evolution on the balance between fidelity of implementation and ease of adoption.

An Evolving Entrepreneurship Simulation as a Vehicle for Career and Technical Education

Edgar E. Troudt, Stuart A. Schulman, Christoph Winkler

To build the skills demanded by the innovation economy education needs to be appropriate to the times (Atkinson & Mayo, 2010), as do the methodologies and strategies employed to teach these skills. The workforce has placed an increasingly large premium on technology skills no matter the occupation. Success in our global, collective future depends upon today's students developing and implementing innovative solutions. These solutions require both changes in thinking and the useful application of these new ideas. Entrepreneurs are those individuals who translate innovation into economic development (Microsoft, 2011a, 2011b).

Increasingly, employment and entrepreneurship will be intertwined as parts of an individual's career pathway and history. These zigzag careers where one frequently changes jobs as opportunities appear, are ever more prevalent (Schulman & Rogoff, 2011). In today's world, according to the Bureau of Labor Statistics (2017), graduates will work for an average of more than 15 employers in the course of their careers. As a result it becomes increasingly important to prepare our future workforce to think and act entrepreneurially in order to be able to respond to the changing demands of the workplace.

In order to illustrate this notion, we explore the Virtual Enterprise (VE), a pedagogical system in which students simulate the conceptualization and operation of an entrepreneurial start-up. VE is interdisciplinary and contextualizes skills from other disciplines (such as those that comprise science, technology, engineering, and mathematics [STEM]) within a business and entrepreneurship framework. We explore the model and

NEW DIRECTIONS FOR COMMUNITY COLLEGES, no. 178, Summer 2017 © 2017 Wiley Periodicals, Inc.
Published online in Wiley Online Library (wileyonlinelibrary.com) • DOI: 10.1002/cc.20251

evolution of the pedagogical system from the perspective of the Institute for Virtual Enterprise (IVE) at the City University of New York (CUNY). This work emphasizes its curricular application in STEM degrees within career and technical education (CTE). Last, we explore funding mechanisms for those adaptations and future efforts at project sustainability.

History: Origins of the Pedagogical System at the Institute for Virtual Enterprise

Today VE, as operated by the CUNY IVE, is a pedagogical system that has student teams conceptualize and operate a simulated business inside a classroom. The pedagogical system comprises a series of experiential learning exercises for groups of students, supporting technological tools and network events. There are other providers of Virtual Enterprise and similarly related practice firms worldwide. However, this paper focuses only on the work of CUNY IVE, which emphasizes an interdisciplinary approach to entrepreneurship education in career fields both STEM and non-STEM related.

The IVE model of Virtual Enterprise started at CUNY's Kingsborough Community College (KCC) as a fully standalone business education course in the Department of Tourism and Hospitality. Students worked together in one or two simulated businesses within a single classroom. The original premise was to teach basic business operation skills (such as accounting, marketing, and sales) as well as general professional skills (such as memo writing, presentations, and effective group work). The semester would culminate with students presenting at a trade show of similar businesses within the VE network at KCC.

In this form, the VE was akin to an internship program with the classroom instructor typically assuming the role as chief executive officer. Over the course of the semester, student teams assumed different leadership positions of the various departments within the simulated company. Operations continued from semester to semester with students leaving instructions for the following cohort. The department had several standard hospitality businesses that continued over the years (Graziano, 2003). The instructor could introduce dynamic events (such as a significant drop in revenue due to an unforeseen incident) via memos to the students. Despite this, the course was rigorously managed with a full semester of exercises, often taking a very predictable path.

Over the years of offerings, innovations to the model began to take hold. Several small grants and support from KCC and CUNY allowed for IVE to develop its own virtual economy known as the Market Maker (www.ivefinancial.com). The Market Maker system is composed of a banking system, an e-commerce platform with an integrated credit card system, and a simulated stock market. With this new flexibility, the tools offered, and a newfound interest in entrepreneurship from the department, the pedagogy was revised to allow for students to conceptualize their own businesses and present these to the larger community of virtual firms on the Market Maker. Over time, the focus of the course went from a simulated internship (learning about the basic office skills required for operating a business) to guiding the creative processes associated with innovation and entrepreneurship.

These pedagogical innovations at KCC served as a catalyst to expanding the VE pedagogies to a variety of other disciplines. Of particular importance were a series of awards by the National Science Foundation's (NSF) Advanced Technological Education (ATE) program (Schulman & Deutsch, 2004; Winkler & Troudt, 2008) that served as a catalyst to bring business and entrepreneurship education into STEM programs; particularly computer science, biotechnology, and electronics.

In order to explore the practical relevance of entrepreneurship to STEM programs in CTE, the next section highlights the relationship between entrepreneurial processes and competencies within a VE pedagogical framework.

The Pedagogical Model of IVE's Virtual Enterprise—Processes and Competencies

The design of IVE's VE builds on action-based entrepreneurship education that is rooted in a specific set of experiences (Neck & Greene, 2011; Neck, Greene, & Brush, 2014). It encompasses learning experiences that emulate high levels of uncertainty in the current economy, innovation, creativity, and entrepreneurship. Thus, the VE is a powerful tool that enables the student entrepreneur to efficiently simulate the process from ideation to actual business launch while developing and applying a broad range of entrepreneurial competencies.

The Process of Entrepreneurial Practice.   A VE simulation allows us to emulate actual entrepreneurial processes in a condensed, accelerated, yet realistic way. To illustrate how VE aligns with existing entrepreneurship processes, we examine how the application of a VE corresponds closely to the Five Practices of Entrepreneurship (adapted from the work of Neck & Greene, 2011; Neck et al., 2014).

The Practice of Creation or Ideation.   The learner engages in the creative process and explores creation rather than prediction. Thus, VE students develop something of value within the space of their academic discipline by applying content expertise with an ability to produce something of value (Dew, Read, Sarasvathy, & Wiltbank, 2009; Neck & Greene, 2011; Sarasvathy, 2008; Schlesinger, Kiefer, & Brown, 2012).

The Practice of Experimentation or Simulation.   Students test their idea in a VE simulation environment. They interact with potential customers to shape the business within their respective discipline. The VE pedagogical system is often augmented and supported by real-world business modeling tools such as Steve Blank's Lean Launchpad (Blank & Dorf, 2012) or The Business Model Canvas (Osterwalder & Pigneur, 2010).

The Practice of Incubation.   Students develop their concepts in a supportive environment with an eye toward launching their venture. Entrepreneurship often requires prototyping, quick testing, and model pivots when faced with obstacles, thus developing an iterative product and market development process. Essential to this process are outside mentors and access to a wide range of expertise in both the underlying discipline and business and entrepreneurship. During this stage, VE students fine tune their business models and apply the most important competencies from their academic discipline, as well as business and entrepreneurship.

The Practice of Acceleration or Launch.   Here, the student entrepreneurs "fly solo" with their venture as participants in the virtual economy, or Market Maker. They retain access to previously acquired information and resources in a nonstructured framework that requires them to actively engage in online trading activities. Students further explore potential "spin-offs" to the real world by converting their simulated business into a real enterprise. These student entrepreneurs are actively engaging in pitch competitions, seeking seed funding, or evaluating various crowdfunding opportunities.

The Practice of Reflection.   Students internalize and extract meaningful lessons from the VE process. Reflection also interacts with the other practices, thereby creating deeper understanding through experiential learning. The purpose of reflection is to encourage deeper learning, making connections and conclusions (Neck et al., 2014).

The Entrepreneurial Competency Model.   The competency-based model presented by Morris and Kaplan (2014) considers competencies as the drivers of entrepreneurship education. It addresses questions about what we want students to know and be able to do and in what way they think. The model suggests "entrepreneurship education can produce desired entrepreneurial outcomes from increased entrepreneurial intention to changed mindsets to the launching of ventures" (Morris & Kaplan, 2014, p. 49). Morris and Kaplan identified 13 entrepreneurial competencies including Opportunity Recognition, Opportunity Assessment, Risk Management/Mitigation, Conveyance of a Compelling Vision, Tenacity/Perseverance, Creative Problem Solving and Imaginativeness, Resource Leveraging, Guerrilla Skills, Value Creation, Maintain Focus While Adapting, Resilience, Self-Efficacy, and Building and Leveraging Entrepreneurial Networks. These competencies are of great importance in the VE because they not only align with various models of 21st Century Learning Skills and Outcomes but also include specific learning outcomes related to entrepreneurship, student motivation, and faculty engagement (Schroeder, 2001).

Linking Practice and Competency Models Through VE.   The practice and competency models presented here should not be viewed as mutually exclusive. Taken together they provide a robust framework for entrepreneurship education in general and for VE in particular. We suggest that VE addresses the multidimensional reality of entrepreneurship programs by presenting a unified approach that links theory to practice for the students who act as entrepreneurs within their own discipline.

Both the practice and competency-based models challenge traditional methods in developing entrepreneurial knowledge, skills, and competence. To develop these skills and competencies the learners need to engage in practice through experiential learning (Kolb & Kolb, 2005). One of most direct ways to achieve this in the classroom is through the use of simulations (Cadotte, 2014), which have a long history in education and have proven to be effective teaching tools due to the realism, control, and task complexity that they provide (Gosen & Washbush, 2004; Stephen, Parente, & Brown, 2002).

Further, experiential learning has led to increased student engagement in the learning process, thereby improving student performance and outcomes (Myers, 2010). Springer and Borthick (2004) have also observed that simulations provide opportunities for students to work on higher order thinking skills, which are essential for business. To be able to think critically involves "the ability to solve problems that cannot be resolved with a high degree of certainty" (Springer & Borthick, 2004, p. 281). Similar findings apply to VE courses, where student engagement has resulted in a natural expansion of their experiential learning spaces. For instance, students spent an additional 3 hours on the development of their VEs outside the classroom for every hour inside the classroom (Schroeder, 2001).

Entrepreneurial simulations benefit greatly by being constructed in an open-ended manner where students' actions in the simulation determine outcomes. This differs from the computer-based model where outcomes are driven by choices provided by the simulation based on previous actions (Schroeder, 2001). A VE simulation is open ended and bridges the practice and competency models by engaging students in ways that condense complex events in a realistic time frame over the course of a semester. Students contribute content expertise as individual actors and team members to achieve jointly developed goals and objectives. They further have the ability to engage in multidiscipline teams, where entrepreneurship students can link up with students from other content areas who are interested in entrepreneurial activities.

The learning environment of a VE is not confined to the actual classroom but also expands to experiential learning activities outside the classroom. For instance, students may conduct actual market research as part of their VE development. As a result, their experiential learning inside the VE simulation is directly linked to real-life feedback, which may also include technology-based crowdsourcing tools and mechanism. Especially the latter has become an integral part of the Market Maker, which now gives VE students the ability to seek feedback about their business ideas through Facebook likes and comments. In addition, VE students can engage in course-related activities that are offered by IVE. Students can engage in IVE's business pitch channel, semiannual online sales presentations, or face-to-face trading days.

Ultimately, the VE acts as a bridge for the student between school and work. It also unifies various approaches posited by entrepreneurship and learning theory into actionable teaching and learning strategies that result in improved student outcomes (Schroeder, 2001).

Evolving Models to VE Adaptations?

The pressure for relevance and targeted workforce preparation has coincided with recognition of the growing importance of entrepreneurship education (Kuratko, 2005). Now more than ever "our role as educators is to unleash the entrepreneurial spirit of our students, cultivate a mindset of practice, and build environments in which practice can occur. In turn, our students can lead more entrepreneurial lives because of their newly found basis for action, appreciation of learning through action and comfort with ambiguity" (Neck et al., 2014, p. 323). Teaching entrepreneurship requires this type of approach both to engage students and motivate them as contributors to today's innovation economy. As Peter Drucker (1985) has noted "Entrepreneurship is neither science nor art. It is a practice" (p. 1).

Unfortunately, developers of pedagogical systems often struggle with the balance between fidelity of implementation and ease of adoption. As yet, our discussion has focused on explaining the entire VE pedagogical system to situations where it could fill a gap. It is our tendency as educators to continue to build newer and more robust versions of our pedagogical systems and to hold on to these precious innovations.

When we at IVE think about long-term sustainability, adoption in individual classrooms is key. As a result, we began to run 2-day annual faculty development workshops on how to implement the VE pedagogy, on-site seminars at interested partner sites, as well as abbreviated training seminars during a variety of workforce, STEM, and entrepreneurship conferences. During these sessions we quickly learned that we had to adjust the "dosage" of our training in order to gain the highest level of adoption possible in support of our growing network of IVE partner institutions.

We quickly learned that a complete adoption of VE curriculum was seldom possible due to institutional, program, and/or curriculum constraints. Most of our training served as a catalyst for early adoptions of the VE pedagogy. Our most successful adaptations of VE have been accomplished through a combination of ongoing mentoring of faculty and the incorporation of discrete portions of the system into existing curricula. Through this disaggregation of the pedagogical system components, instructors could now use those elements that they felt most comfortable with and that served their classroom the best. And as they gained experience and comfort, these same instructors could adopt more pieces of the program. By experimenting with derivatives that used parts of the pedagogical system, VE moved from a regimented to a modular system.

Faculty in STEM disciplines have been particularly receptive to this development and approach of the VE pedagogical system. These instructors of traditionally research-oriented disciplines were allowed to infuse some exercises in innovation and entrepreneurship, without needing to eliminate core course content or making use of tools that they would be uncomfortable with and that were wholly irrelevant to course outcomes. This infusion model has worked the best for STEM faculty and we were able to build a community of VE adopters thanks to funding from NSF for these initiatives.[1] For instance, we worked with community college faculty across the United States in the disciplinary content areas of information technology, biotechnology, geology, maritime, underwater robotics, and electronics. Building on this work, it is our goal at IVE to share our work and invite interested educators to engage in an ongoing conversation about entrepreneurship education in order to build a community of educational innovators in career and technical education.

Program Sustainability and Future Directions

The future for sustainability and scalability is the lowering and distribution of the labor required for adapting the pedagogy to new disciplines and situations. As previously noted, the VE pedagogical system is training and labor intensive and often requires the participation of partners. In this section, we discuss the plan to lower barriers through automated training and providing rich classroom materials that augment instructor expertise—a reality video series. Next we discuss future plans to expand the concrete guides to implementation in different areas, rigorous documentation of successes, and further flexibility for the tools of the pedagogical system.

Systematizing Training Through a Video Series of the STEM VE. Recognizing the impact of the annual seminar as well as its limited scalability and geographic reach, the institute sought another tool to maximize impact. Through funding from the NSF we have begun development on a video series that follows the processes students undertake in their STEM VE classrooms. For students, the videos will demonstrate model business and entrepreneurial activities they subsequently undertake in class. For faculty members and administrators, instructors will be shown how to add entrepreneurial exercises to STEM classroom activities as well as being provided background information on business processes with which they (as scientists and technologists) may be less familiar.

Future Sustainability: Incubating Action Research. The STEM Virtual Enterprise project was a highly labor-intensive project that verified the feasibility of offering the VE pedagogical system in different disciplines and yielded several high-quality implementation guides. But the team at IVE alone does not have the resources nor the labor force to repeat this intense materials development for the myriad of other educational situations that exist.

Thus, applying the solution of crowdsourcing through commissioning action research studies is a way of distributing labor and putting tasks in the hands of the experts. IVE has begun to plan for recruiting a diverse set of faculty members from a wide variety of institutions and disciplines, providing them with a baseline training in the entrepreneurship education and asking them to implement and study the practices in their own classroom. Participants will be provided incentives through concrete opportunities to study their own teaching and author scholarly publications. This literature, in turn, will be more varied in the types of classrooms, use cases, and disciplines, making the work of future generations of implementers simpler.

Introducing Intelligent Feature Sets.   If the institute's programs are to expand further, more automated algorithms need to be introduced that unbind instructors from traditional semesters and event calendars. Thus far, events in the VE network are sustained through classroom partnerships and classroom-to-classroom transactions at timed intervals. But these synchronous events are complicated by time zones, nonconformity of semester calendars, and varied speed of progression in the business development process between classes. Further, as disaggregation and innovative uses of the technology occur, desire to use certain tools no longer comes at predictable times of the year.

In 2014, IVE began the process of developing a gamification strategy for the business development process. Gamification turns rote processes— for example, exercise or parking—into a competition where rewards are attached to beneficial behaviors. Rewards often come in two forms: accolades (sometimes referred to as "badges") or points of varying magnitude (with an accompanying competitive board sometimes known as a "leader board"). To turn entrepreneurship education into a semiautomated system of rewards, we must dissect the actions of an entrepreneur. These come from the pedagogical model (including process and competencies) previously presented. Then actions, such as refining a business model in response to peer suggestions or seeking advice from an appropriate mentor, will be assigned rewards of an appropriate magnitude. These magnitudes are guided by the difficulty of the task and its likely impact on success.

Conclusion: A Responsibility for Educational Innovation

The VE pedagogical system, especially when applied to CTE and STEM education, is attuned to that workplace into which our students are graduating. Its active learning platform and emphasis on entrepreneurial competencies provide the necessary agility to successfully navigate the challenges that they will face. As educators we owe it to our students to use those strategies that are most effective to succeed entrepreneurially in that "zigzag" workforce that constitutes our innovation economy.

As was demonstrated in the evolution of VE, educational programs should embrace long-term change in incremental steps. Great ideas can start as small yet viable programs. These programs then develop a track record of successful offerings while incrementally recognizing opportunities for growth. Such opportunities may come from adapting the work to new educational levels or disciplines. Other opportunities come from gap analyses that form the basis of funding proposals. And finally, some opportunities come from being able to logically segment your program into discrete building blocks. Individual blocks may be more valuable than the whole to other adopters in achieving their educational mission.

Sustainability is not about repeatedly seeking funding for the same project. The goal is to be creative in the application of your work and think of other audiences that may benefit from your innovations. We invite the readers of this article to join this conversation and to jointly improve our own practice in STEM and other programs across the CTE spectrum.

Note

1. This material is based upon work supported by the National Science Foundation under grant numbers 0501711, 0802365, 1104183, and 1205031. Any opinions, findings, and conclusions or recommendations expressed in this material are those of the authors and do not necessarily reflect the views of the National Science Foundation.

References

Atkinson, R. D., & Mayo, M. J. (2010). *Refueling the US innovation economy: Fresh approaches to science, technology, engineering and mathematics (STEM) education*. Washington, DC: Information Technology & Innovation Foundation. Retrieved from https://ssrn.com/abstract=1722822

Blank, S., & Dorf, B. (2012). *The startup owner's manual: The step-by-step guide for building a great company*. Pescadero, CA: K & S Ranch.

Bureau of Labor Statistics (2017). "National Longitudinal Surveys." https://www.bls.gov/nls/nlsfaqs.htm. Accessed on March 8, 2017.

Cadotte, E. (2014). The use of simulations in entrepreneurship education: Opportunities, challenges and outcomes. In M. H. Morris (Ed.), *Annals of entrepreneurship education and pedagogy* (pp. 280–302). Northampton, MA: Edward Elgar Publishing.

CUNY Institute for Virtual Enterprise. Retrieved from www.ive.cuny.edu.

Dew, N., Read, S., Sarasvathy, S. D., & Wiltbank, R. (2009). Effectual versus predictive logics in entrepreneurial decision-making: Differences between experts and novices. *Journal of Business Venturing*, 24(4), 287–309.

Dickson, P. H., Solomon, G. T., & Weaver, K. M. (2008). Entrepreneurial selection and success: does education matter?. *Journal of Small business and enterprise development*, 15(2), 239–258.

Drucker, P. (1985). *Innovation and entrepreneurship*. New York: Harper & Row.

Gosen, J., & Washbush, J. (2004). A review of scholarship on assessing experiential learning effectiveness. *Simulation & Gaming*, 35(2), 270–293.

Graziano, R. (2003). *Students' perceptions of an experiential, active learning strategy for business and career education* (Unpublished doctoral dissertation). Hofstra University, Hempstead, NY.

Kolb, A. Y., & Kolb, D. A. (2005). Learning styles and learning spaces: Enhancing experiential learning in higher education. *Academy of Management Learning & Education*, 4(2), 193–212.

Kuratko, D. F. (2005). The emergence of entrepreneurship education: Development, trends, and challenges. *Entrepreneurship Theory and Practice*, 29(5), 577–598.

Microsoft. (2011a). *Building a culture of entrepreneurship—Starting with education.*

Microsoft. (2011b). *Employability, entrepreneurship and workforce development.*

Morris, M. H., & Kaplan, J. (2014) Entrepreneurial (versus managerial) competencies as drivers of entrepreneurship education. In M. H. Morris (Ed.), *Annals of entrepreneurship education and pedagogy* (pp. 134–151). Northampton, MA: Edward Elgar Publishing.

Myers, S. D. (2010). Experiential learning and consumer behavior: An exercise in consumer decision making. *Journal for Advancement of Marketing Education*, 17(1), 23–26.

Neck, H. M., & Greene, P. G. (2011). Entrepreneurship education: known worlds and new frontiers. *Journal of Small Business Management*, 49(1), 55–70.

Neck, H. M., Greene, P. G., & Brush, C. G. (2014). *Practice-based entrepreneurship education using actionable theory.* In M. H. Morris (Ed.), *Annals of entrepreneurship education and pedagogy* (pp. 3–20). Northampton, MA: Edward Elgar Publishing.

Osterwalder, A., & Pigneur, Y. (2010). *Business model generation: a handbook for visionaries, game changers, and challengers.* New York: John Wiley & Sons.

Sarasvathy, S. D. (2008). *Effectuation: Elements of entrepreneurial expertise*, Cheltenham, UK & Northampton, MA: Edward Elgar.

Schlesinger, L. A., Kiefer, C. F., & Brown, P. B. (2012). *Just start: Take action, embrace uncertainty, create the future.* Cambridge, MA: Harvard Business Press.

Schroeder, B. (2001). *Kingsborough Community College Virtual Enterprises: Case study, formative evaluation.* New York, NY: City University of New York, Center for Advanced Study in Education.

Schulman, S. A., & Deutsch, J. (2004). *Virtual Information Technology Enterprises (VEIT): An Integrated Vehicle for Technology Reform.* National Science Foundation Grant (NSF/ATE DUE-0802365).

Schulman, S. A., & Rogoff, E. G. (2011). The technology enabled entrepreneur: Today's hope for a better tomorrow. *Entrepreneurship Research Journal*, 1(4). doi: https://doi.org/10.2202/2157-5665.1057

Springer, C. W., & Borthick, A. F. (2004). Business simulation to stage critical thinking in introductory accounting: Rationale, design, and implementation. *Issues in Accounting Education*, 19(3), 277–303.

Stephen, J., Parente, D. H., & Brown, R. C. (2002). Seeing the forest and the trees: Balancing functional and integrative knowledge using large-scale simulations in capstone business strategy classes. *Journal of Management Education*, 26(2), 164–193.

Winkler, C., & Troudt, E. E. (2008). Enhancing Soft and Entrepreneurial Skills Training for Two-Year College Technicians Using a Contextualized Business Simulation Program. National Science Foundation Grant (NSF ATE DUE- 0802365).

EDGAR E. TROUDT *is assistant dean for research and strategic partnerships at Long Island University - Brooklyn.*

STUART A. SCHULMAN *is professor of management in the Loomba Department of Management at Baruch College, CUNY.*

CHRISTOPH WINKLER *is associate professor in entrepreneurship at Long Island University - Brooklyn.*

This chapter summarizes funding trends to support career and technical education (CTE) and science, technology, engineering, and math (STEM) programs at community colleges compared to funding for similar programs at 4-year colleges and universities. Examples of intramural and extramural funding strategies as well as lessons learned and implications of funding innovations are shared focusing on STEM and CTE programs.

How Community Colleges Are Closing the Skills Gap Through CTE and STEM Funding Innovations

Kimberly Lowry, Tricia Thomas-Anderson

According to Christopher Mullin (2010a), one of the missions of the community college is to provide access to, and opportunity for, education through courses that serve as the foundation for a career, a new life, or a new perspective. Course offerings at community colleges demonstrating the greatest economic impact in the United States are often those associated with career and technical education (CTE) and STEM programs. Community colleges also play a major role in workforce training programs that offer both credit and noncredit courses leading to industry-based certification. Many of these certifications require basic and sometimes advanced STEM skills. Although the acronym STEM is fairly specific in nature—referring to science, technology, engineering, and math—there is no standard definition for what constitutes a STEM job. Uniquely positioned to develop the pipeline of STEM professionals and produce more STEM-skilled workers to meet the demand for middle- and high-skill jobs, community colleges are also an inexpensive option for the many low-income, low-skilled adults who want and need to boost their education and training. Surprisingly, according to Jim Brazell (2013), the highest earnings for STEM workers are for those with less than a college degree.

According to several vocational educators and subject matter experts, high-quality career and technical education programs as well as STEM pathways prepare students for high-demand occupations (Brown, 2003; Drage,

New Directions for Community Colleges, no. 178, Summer 2017 © 2017 Wiley Periodicals, Inc.
Published online in Wiley Online Library (wileyonlinelibrary.com) • DOI: 10.1002/cc.20252

45

2009). These programs and pathways also have the capacity to launch America's future global competitiveness by emphasizing increased student engagement and innovative integration of traditional academic courses, meeting the needs of both employers and the economy as a whole (Brown, 2003; Drage, 2009). Shifting economic and societal trends have reinvented the role of higher education into a resource for students looking for accelerated pathways into the workplace and for employers looking for defined skill sets to fill jobs filled with high school graduates. As a result, the rapid evolution of the workforce means that employers are increasingly turning to community colleges as essential centers of CTE and STEM worker training. As reported by the U.S. Department of Commerce's Economics and Statistics Administration, in 2010, there were 7.6 million STEM workers in the United States, representing about 1 in 18 workers. Over the past 10 years, growth in STEM jobs was three times as fast as growth in non-STEM jobs. STEM occupations are projected to grow by 17.0% from 2008 to 2018, compared to 9.8% growth for non-STEM occupations (Langdon, McKittrick, Beede, Khan, & Doms, 2014). As workforce and employers' needs continue to rise at a rapid pace, the need for community colleges to offer worker-related training and have the financial resources needed to pay for it is more important than ever in closing the skills gap.

How Funding Community Colleges Closes the Skills Gap

Community colleges have played an essential role of providing an opportunity for individuals who have not fully enjoyed economic possibilities of America, such as ethnic/racial minorities, people with disabilities, individuals with limited English proficiency (LEP), and those lacking adequate academic preparation for postsecondary persistence and completion. According to Budd and Hawkins (2002), community colleges are the most responsive segment of higher education in meeting the immediate needs of local communities and are vital to sustaining the competitive edge of North America in the 21st century. Community colleges do this in one way by supporting economic growth with CTE programs that focus on providing potential employees with the skills necessary to meet the workforce development needs of regional employers in emerging and expanding industries.

Formerly referred to as "vocational education," career and technical education has witnessed a movement since 2011 emphasizing integration with STEM and vocational practice in programs of study (Gasbarre, 2007). As a result, educational organizations have developed and maintained STEM and CTE networks across the United States to link high school, community college, and university academic pathways with careers. These networks are emerging but stumble with limited funding and leadership.

Just as Budd and Hawkins (2002) introduced their research with the words of former U.S. Secretary of Labor, Robert Reich, "community colleges are the unsung heroes of our workforce development system" (p. 1),

NEW DIRECTIONS FOR COMMUNITY COLLEGES • DOI: 10.1002/cc

with state and other funding resources, community colleges are able to serve business and industry by training technical workers; serving regional employers by adapting quickly to changing conditions in local workforce needs; offering customized training to technical workers; providing certification training in support of new technologies; and delivering education and training wherever and whenever they are needed. However, career and technical as well as STEM education can be extremely expensive for community colleges, requiring a greater devotion of resources (Budd and Hawkins, 2002) and innovative ways to obtain funding.

Ways to Obtain Funding for STEM-Related Career and Technical Education

The majority of career and technical education programs require advanced technologies in order to ensure students enrolled have access to comprehensive instruction and laboratory experiences in high-demand career pathways. With the exception of internal funding allocations from the institution's annual budget or intramural development funding to support faculty innovations, most community colleges depend heavily on external funding for career and technical education. For example, under the Carl D. Perkins Career and Technical Education Improvement Act, the Workforce Innovation Opportunity Act, and other work-ready initiatives offered through the U.S. Department of Labor, the U.S. government allocates grant funding specifically for workforce programs. Community colleges, like other educational institutions, also receive noncompetitive public funding allocations as a percentage of their internal budgets to fund expenditures as well as support academic programs and success among these and other students.

Internal or Intramural Funding. According to Mullin (2010b) the fastest growing expenditure categories among community colleges are in areas that ensure institutions have the capacity to meet students' growing needs for career guidance, counseling, and other support as well as the increasing costs of marketing and general administrative expenses. Based on a needs survey conducted by the Education Commission of the States and Community Policy Center (2000), public funding for community colleges, particularly from state and local governments, has declined by nearly 30% since 2000 and there are no clear signs of the reversal of that trend. Ironically, this decrease in funding for basic support of community colleges continues as the contribution of community colleges to the public interest appears to have increased.

According to Dowd and Shieh (2013), at present, state and local government appropriations are the largest internal funding sources for community colleges. State and local government appropriations comprise over 41% of community college revenue. In addition to state and local government allocations, 16% of revenue sources derive from tuition and fees. These dollars, as well as 4% of revenue sources from activity sales and services (such as fees for attending athletics) total over 60% of community college's revenue and internal funding (Dowd & Shieh, 2013). As institutions strategically determine how and where the annual budget should be allocated, division leaders often are required to advocate for and justify necessary dollars designed to enhance and/or expand instructional programs, including those that are CTE and STEM focused. As a result, internal funding for program growth commonly requires a formal request, in some form, in order to maximize the efficiency of dollars invested with limited resources. Although not always as formally competitive as external funding requests to government and private funding agencies, internal funding requests, where funding is limited, encourages a somewhat competitive environment.

External or Extramural Funding. Trends in total institution revenue for community colleges indicate significant shifts toward external revenue sources and away from core state and local funding for basic operations. As a matter of fact, the share of total revenue for community colleges attributed to federal and state agencies, corporations, and individuals grew from 2% in 1980 to 20% in 1996, an 18% increase in less than 2 decades. Dowd and Shied also reported that operating and other external grants comprised approximately 31% of total revenue for community colleges, demonstrating the continued increase in external funding pursuits to support operating and nonoperating expenditures. Unlike 4-year universities, the authors' findings regarding funding trends from peer-reviewed literature and studies revealed that 2-year colleges have been the least likely identified as eligible recipients of intramural and/or extramural funding commonly offered by agencies interested in supporting STEM-related research and education. However, to address the gap in external funding supporting 2-year institutions of higher education, in 2010, legislators implemented an Obama administration proposal—the American Graduation Initiative (AGI)—that would have invested roughly 12 billion dollars in community colleges over 10 years, with the goal of greatly improving students' performance and increasing the number of community college graduates by 5 million dollars over that time. Community colleges initiated grant initiatives that would be managed by the U.S. Department of Labor to help dislocated workers access training programs.

The Trade Adjustment Assistance Community College and Career Training (TAACCCT) initiative promotes skills development and employment opportunities in fields such as advanced manufacturing, transportation, and health care, as well as science, technology, engineering, and math careers through partnerships between training providers and local employers. The Department of Labor is implementing and administering the program in coordination with the Department of Education. The grants include 27 awards to community college and university consortia totaling $359,237,048 and 27 awards to individual institutions totaling $78,262,952 (U.S. Department of Labor, 2012). U.S. Department of Labor TAACCCT grantees are using problem- and project-based approaches to create rigorous programs focused on high-STEM careers, engaging employers in program design, creating career-coaching systems, and helping students attain key mathematics and literacy skills. The grant funding also helps community colleges and other eligible institutions develop, offer, or improve education and career training programs suitable for workers eligible for Trade Adjustment Assistance.

Like the TAACCCT program, initiatives funded by the National Science Foundation's Advanced Technological Education (ATE) program are addressing the skills gap challenge nationwide. The ATE program is working to "prepare technicians for the high-technology workplaces that the United States needs to prosper." Thirty-nine ATE centers and many ATE-funded projects are using innovative approaches to tackle workforce preparation issues through strategic partnerships among K–12 education, secondary CTE, 2- and 4-year colleges, and employers (STEM Smart, 2014).

In addition to the Department of Labor, other agencies such as the National Science Foundation, the Department of Education, the Health Resources and Services Administration, the National Endowment for the Humanities, the Institute of International Education, and state governments are earmarking funding for initiatives specifically to support community colleges in their roles of closing the skills gap through CTE and STEM-related programs. Additionally, although several have as their purpose targeting skills development for low-wage workers and increased completion rates for students enrolled at a community college, not all agency initiatives are specifically targeting college students and industry trainees. For example, the Texas Education Agency, Texas Higher Education Coordinating Board, and Texas Workforce Commission developed a collaborative and each committed funding to support innovative education partnerships between local school districts and public community or technical colleges for the development of four new career and technical education early college high school (CTE ECHS) opportunities for students in Dallas, Houston, McAllen, and Odessa. The goal of the CTE ECHS program is to enable students to be immediately employable by providing them with job skills and an opportunity to earn stackable credentials that include Level II certificates, at least 60 credit hours toward an associate of applied science (AAS) degree or an AAS degree. These STEM-integrated CTE programs of study include machining, digital media technology, computer-aided drafting and design, manufacturing/ mechatronics technology, industrial electricity, health information technology, and more (Texas Higher Education Coordinating Board, 2014).

The Texas Workforce Commission (2014) also funded colleges for the expansion of career and technical dual-credit programs from its Skills Development Fund grants to support certain joint-credit courses offered by school districts in partnership with public junior colleges, public state colleges, or public technical institutions. The legislature made available

$450,000 to further support the creation and expansion of dual-credit career and technical education in Texas schools that are highly technical in nature, addressing local area demands for high-skill, high-demand, and high-wage industries. The grant allows training of high school students in dual-credit curriculum to be used toward a Level I, industry-recognized technical certificate.

Outside of government funding opportunities, corporate and private foundations have also recognized the value of investing in business and technology partnerships with community colleges to establish and implement work-ready programs and skills development projects. For example, J.P. Morgan Chase recently invested 250 million dollars in partnerships with major urban cities across the nation to implement projects that align with the corporation's New Skills at Work initiative, designed to minimize the skills gap among individuals currently employed as well as those seeking employment in an increasingly technical workforce (Wright, 2013).

Lessons Learned and Implications

Access, open enrollment, and affordability have become staples of the mission of community colleges. However, with costs and funding justifications in higher education changing rapidly and varying considerably by state, identifying secondary funding sources has become more important than ever. According to the Century Foundation Taskforce of Preventing Community Colleges from Becoming Separate and Unequal (2013), between academic years 1999 and 2009, every 4-year sector saw increases, whereas community college funding was flat. During this 10-year period, at the extremes, private research sector expenditures increased by $13,912, whereas public community colleges saw a rise of just $1.

The Obama administration has made substantial headway in promoting industry partnerships to foster career readiness and job creation for trained workers through the Community College to Career Fund as well as other opportunities for increased funding for the development and expansion of career and technical education programs. However, more has to be done to sustain these efforts. According to Lindsey-Taliefero and Tucker (2013), addressing this problem must be done collaboratively by college administrators, faculty, staff, public officials, and legislative liaisons to successfully attain funding support from their respective state legislators. For example, CTE is now one of the principal components included in Essential Programs and Services (EPS), the state of Maine's model for funding public education. This new model provided an increased funding source for state and local equipment expenditures for instructional purposes and is similar to provisions developed in other states, such as Missouri, Virginia, and Pennsylvania, to support funding of equipment for CTE programs (Allen, 2009).

Community colleges help prepare an exceedingly diverse population of students for a wide array of careers, including STEM and CTE occupations, yet face complex challenges. In fact, according to STEM Smart (2014) and the National Academies Summit of 2011, supported by the National Science Foundation (NSF), finding the resources to support and sustain STEM education program improvement is one of the primary challenges community colleges face. Traditionally, states have funded higher education based on enrollments and prior-year spending. However, some states are experimenting with community college funding based on output measures such as degree completion, on-time course-sequence completion, and transfer rates to 4-year institutions. At a minimum, such performance-based funding should be substantial enough to get colleges' attention and change the way they allocate resources to promote student completion of programs of study. In fact, research indicates that at least 5% of base state funding—in addition to new money—could be allocated on the basis of course- and degree-completion measures. Focusing these efforts on target populations and STEM is a way for states to reward community colleges for increasing STEM course-completion rates.

As community colleges continue to serve a growing number of students, another major concern is that the credits students are earning at community colleges do not lead to a useful certificate or degree or facilitate the students' successful transfer to a 4-year college. In many cases, even when credits are transferable, STEM course credits are counted as electives by 4-year institutions. Variability in community college program quality and a lack of articulation agreements between 2- and 4-year colleges are major contributors to this problem. A similar dilemma exists regarding industry credentials. Students and workers are investing time and money earning certificates or credentials that do not have college credits associated with them. These credits many times are not recognized outside of local sector-specific labor markets and cannot be applied to continued learning opportunities.

Finally, according to Angela Baber (2011), the increasing need for community colleges to remediate students, particularly in mathematics, is a growing concern. Mathematics is the most common remedial course taken. A recent study reported by George Boggs (2012) found only one third of students referred to remedial math courses ever complete the recommended developmental courses. Even fewer of these students go on to pass a credit-bearing mathematics course. Students, as well as adults already in the education and workforce system, need better math remediation options at the community college level to become qualified for STEM-related jobs.

Conclusion

According to the Education Commission of the States and Community College Policy Center (2000), in the area of CTE, states tend to rely on three types of revenue sources to fund workforce development: (a) specific funds dedicated to workforce development activities included as part of the state appropriation to community colleges; (b) other state funding sources for which community colleges can apply to support these activities; and (c) nonstate funding sources for which community colleges also may apply. Several external funding opportunities are emerging specifically designed to support and enhance community college programs where community colleges have the potential to encourage enrollment and completion particularly in career and technical education programs. However, beyond external grant funding opportunities to support specific projects, community college operating budgets seldom include funding to support projects designed to enhance research and/or programs of study in career and technical education internally.

Lack of appropriate funding for community colleges is obviously a major challenge if they are to be responsible for closing the skills gap. The theoretical justification for the differing levels of funding within our system of higher education is that it allows different institutions to focus on what they do best. Four-year institutions will attract the most highly prepared students, the theory suggests, and 2-year institutions will educate large numbers of less prepared students to their own levels of success. Contrary to this belief, the reality is, thousands of jobs within American industries have been outsourced to other countries as a result of the United States' negligence and limited support of the development of students enrolled in community colleges and career and technical education programs (Halls, 2009). The demand for students and workers who are able to think critically and solve real-world problems is increasing. At the same time, different students learn differently.

Traditional community college programs generally engage students in narrow and limited ways that do not cultivate the problem-solving abilities critical to success in a growing number of professions resulting in the existence of insufficient training models at many community colleges. Additionally, completion rates for community college courses also are woefully low. The many contributing factors include a lack of coherent curriculum, lack of guidance toward course completion, and a disconnection between programs and employment opportunities. STEM courses, in particular, tend to be undersupplied and enrollment restricted because they are more expensive. Additionally, as Mullin's (2010a) research suggests, without the funding support necessary to adequately offer CTE programs, community colleges are forced to turn away students interested in enrolling in high-demand workforce programs due to lack of space, credentialed instructors, and/or appropriate equipment, which ultimately continues to stunt the country's workforce development and economic growth. The good news is that, although limited, innovative ways to obtain funding do exist and community colleges are now more important than ever. Furthermore, through the thoughtful investment in STEM-intensive CTE programs, the United States can readily increase its supply of motivated and prepared students entering STEM-related fields and strengthen the general STEM literacy of the emerging U.S. workforce.

References

Allen, D. (2009). *Funding for career and technical education*. Portland, ME: Maine Education Policy Research Institute, University of Southern Maine.

Baber, A. (2011). *Using community colleges to build a STEM skilled workforce*. Washington, DC: National Governors Association, Center for Best Practices.

Boggs, G. (2012). *POV: Community colleges and STEM education*. Washington, DC: American Association of Community Colleges.

Brazell, J. (2013). STEM 2.0: Transformational Thinking about STEM for Education and Career Practitioners. *Career Planning and Adult Development Journal*, 29(2), 20-33

Brown, B. L. (2003). *Connecting CTE to labor market information*. Columbus, OH: Ohio State University, Center on Education and Training for Employment. Retrieved from ERIC database. (ED479341).

Budd, S., & Hawkins, J. (2002). *Investing in people and strengthening communities through support of community colleges: A case for funding* (New Century Series Resource Paper #4). Silver Spring, MD: Council of Resource Development.

Century Foundation Taskforce of Preventing Community Colleges from Becoming Separate and Unequal. (2013). *Bridging the higher education divide: Strengthening community colleges and restoring the American dream*. New York, NY: Century Foundation Press.

Dowd, A. C., & Shieh, L. T. (2013). Community college financing: Equity, efficiency, and accountability. *National Education Association (NEA) 2013 Almanac on Higher Education*, 37–65.

Drage, K. (2009). Modernizing career and technical education programs. *Techniques: Connecting Education and Careers*, 84(5), 32–34.

Education Commission of the States & Community College Policy Center. (2000). *State funding for community colleges: A 50-state survey*. Denver, CO: Author.

Gasbarre, A. D. (2007). Vocational education. Retrieved from http://www.reference forbusiness.com/encyclopedia/Val-Z/Vocational-Education.html

Halls, N. (2009). How valuable is CTE in this economy? *Techniques: Association for Career and Technical Education*, 83(9), 62.

Langdon, D., McKittrick, G., Beede, D., Khan, B., & Doms, M. (2014). *STEM: Good jobs now and for the future*. Washington, DC: U.S. Department of Commerce, Economics and Statistics Administration, Office of the Chief Economist.

Lindsey-Taliefero, D., & Tucker, L. (2013). Community college funding: Legislators' attitudes. *Creative Education*, 4(11), 694.

Mullin, C. M. (2010a). *Doing more with less: The inequitable funding of community colleges*. Washington, DC: American Association of Community Colleges.

Mullin, C. M. (2010b). *Rebalancing the mission: The community college completion challenge* (Policy Brief 2010-02PBL). Washington, DC: American Association of Community Colleges.

STEM Smart. (2014). *CTE pathways to STEM occupations*. Washington, DC: Community for Advancing Discovery Research in Education (CADRE), Education Development Center.

Texas Higher Education Coordinating Board. (2014). *Texas education, higher education and workforce agencies award innovative education-to-workforce program grants: Dallas, Houston, McAllen and Odessa to launch new career and technical education early college high school programs* [Press release]. Retrieved from http://www. thecb.state.tx.us/download.cfm?downloadfile=A1CF9824-FBAC-07CD-99E39988 30CA4698&typename=dmFile&fieldname=filename

Texas Workforce Commission. (2014). *Area school districts partner with North Central Texas College for $195,258 dual-credit grant* [Press release]. Retrieved from http://www.twc.state.tx.us/files/news/pressrelease-02122015-area-school-districts-partner-with-north-central-college-grant-twc.pdf

U.S. Department of Labor. (2012). *Obama administration announces $500 million in community college grants to expand job training through local employer partnerships: Grants are the second installment of $2 billion, 4-year initiative* [Press release]. Retrieved fromhttp://www.dol.gov/opa/media/press/eta/ETA20121885.htm

Wright, J. (2013). Analyzing local skills gaps as part of JPMorgan Chase's "New Skills at Work" initiative. Retrieved from http://www.economicmodeling.com/2013/12/12/analyzing-local-skills-gaps-as-part-of-jpmorgan-chases-new-skills-at-work-initiative/

KIMBERLY LOWRY *is associate vice president of academic affairs and student success at Eastfield College of the Dallas County Community College District.*

TRICIA THOMAS-ANDERSON *is dean of resource development at Eastfield College of the Dallas County Community College District.*

NEW DIRECTIONS FOR COMMUNITY COLLEGES • DOI: 10.1002/cc

5

When linked to program review and improvement, program evaluation can help practitioners to ensure that career-technical education (CTE) and science, technology, engineering, and mathematics (STEM) programs offer equitable access and outcomes for underserved student groups.

The Case for Evaluating Student Outcomes and Equity Gaps to Improve Pathways and Programs of Study

Debra D. Bragg

New approaches to program evaluation are needed to ensure that career-technical education (CTE) and science, technology, engineering, and mathematics (STEM) education is assessing outcomes, improving programs, and demonstrating accountability. CTE has a long history of federal funding for program evaluation; however, measures and indicators have been inconsistently and inaccurately applied, and evaluation methods have varied widely (Klein et al., 2014). Changes are needed to ensure that program evaluation can assess the outcomes of all learner groups and contribute to program improvement. By emphasizing the way evaluation can assess outcomes for student subgroups, including disaggregating outcomes for students historically underserved by postsecondary education, it will be possible for program evaluation to produce information that closes equity gaps in access and outcomes.

This chapter begins with a description of how federal CTE legislation has conceived of evaluation for the purpose of program review and improvement. The discussion highlights an approach to program improvement that began in Illinois, called Pathways to Results, that integrates equity and outcomes assessment into local CTE program improvement. Demonstrating how practitioners use data to improve programs and enhance learner outcomes, the chapter ends with implications for evaluating both CTE and STEM education programs in the future.

New Directions for Community Colleges, no. 178, Summer 2017 © 2017 Wiley Periodicals, Inc.
Published online in Wiley Online Library (wileyonlinelibrary.com) • DOI: 10.1002/cc.20253

Evaluation of Career-Technical Education

Federal policy on CTE has emphasized program evaluation for the purposes of performance reporting, accountability, and program improvement for decades. Released more than 10 years ago, the National Assessment of Vocational Education (NAVE; Silverberg, Warner, Fong, & Goodwin, 2004) report laid the groundwork for the current federal Carl D. Perkins Career and Technical Education Act of 2006, known as Perkins IV. Indeed, NAVE's comprehensive report on the 1998 Carl D. Perkins Vocational and Applied Technology Education Act (known as Perkins III) showed that postsecondary vocational education (now called career-technical education or CTE) had extensive national reach in terms of enrolling an estimated one third of all undergraduate students (and one half of all high school students), but these diverse individuals participated in highly varied ways to achieve different ends. Students who took more high school-level academic course work in conjunction with CTE classes tended to perform better than those taking fewer academic classes and CTE. Gender differences were detected in vocational course participation aligned with occupations stratified on income (e.g., early childhood and health care for females, manufacturing and information technology for males).

Although indicative of inequities among student groups, these results lack the kind of specificity that practitioners need to improve programs, calling for evaluation methods that disaggregate student outcomes by subgroup. This finding is further complicated by the fact that Perkins III dismantled set-asides for some special populations, including gender (e.g., elimination of the set-aside for state gender equity), coupled with fewer requirements for local agencies to direct funds to schools and programs that serve large proportions of special populations.

To this point, Silverberg et al. (2004, p. 15) noted a "weakening" of funding for high-poverty communities due to increased flexibility in funding provisions in the 1998 federal law. They also cautioned that the potential funding advantage that Perkins III intended for high-poverty districts was not realized in some districts; in fact, the extent to which CTE programs had served high-poverty districts declined since the 1990 federal law on vocational education was put in effect between 1990 and 1998. Whereas the federal accountability effort associated with Perkins III raised state-level commitment to accountability in some ways, state-supported program evaluation was weakened in other ways, with diminished emphasis on valid and reliable performance measures and inconsistencies in data collection and reporting being a primary contributor. Silverberg et al. ultimately concluded state systems could not "provide a reliable, national picture of vocational education performance" (p. 242). The problem of data quality was even more problematic at the local level where relatively few districts could implement robust approaches to program evaluation.

In 2006, the Carl D. Perkins Career and Technical Education Act (P.L. 109–270) was passed, representing continued federal commitment to CTE. Placing more emphasis on program improvement and accountability than the previous law, Perkins IV strengthened its focus on performance measures tied to the renewal of CTE programs of study. This law required that all states integrate academic and CTE subject matter into coherent programs of study. Students who participate in these programs are expected to follow a career pathway approach that assists them to transition from high school to postsecondary education and employment. In light of this policy, CTE researchers funded by the U.S. Department of Education grappled with ways to ensure that program evaluation would be strengthened in the current context. They observed that resources awarded through federal CTE funding have never been sufficient to address the immensity of state and national evaluation needs and that they were stretched even further under Perkins IV.

Kotamraju (2010) led an initiative for the National Center for Career and Technical Education (NCCTE) to improve program evaluation and accountability, including recommending a clearer definition of what it means to be a CTE student and meaningful measures of "the boundaries of his or her experiences" (p. 50). His working group recognized the importance of centering program evaluation on clear definitions of who participates in CTE programs so that it would be possible to attribute outcomes to student groups. Moreover, Kotamraju recommended that the federal government and states develop a standard data system to track CTE students' progression into and through career pathways and programs of study to employment, with measures that convey student performance at major milestones and completion points. In calling for this change, Kotamraju recognized that student trajectories are not linear, noting students move back and forth between education and employment. He urged policymakers to take these complex patterns of enrollment and employment into account when measuring and interpreting student outcomes, in order to understand the impact of CTE programs.

In a closely related initiative, the National Association of State Directors of Career Technical Education Consortium (NASDCTEc) endorsed widespread dissemination of the National Career Cluster Framework that classifies occupations and industries according to career clusters, career pathways, and programs of study. This Career Cluster Framework provides a useful structure for program evaluation of CTE, though it does not appear to be used in this manner very often. Consistent with Perkins IV, this framework provides a means of classifying programs of study to assess whether they are meeting federal requirements to:

- Incorporate and align secondary and postsecondary education elements
- Include academic and CTE content in a coordinated, nonduplicative progression of courses

- Offer the opportunity, where appropriate, for secondary students to acquire postsecondary credits.lead to an industry-recognized credential or certificate at the postsecondary level, or an associate or baccalaureate degree

Closely aligned is the Common Career and Technical Core (CCTC) that specifies common benchmarks that states should use to assess what students should know and be able to do after completing a program of study. Another framework of use to program evaluation is the Program of Study Design Framework that identifies 10 essential components that support implementation of CTE programs of study (POS), which are:

1. Legislation and policies
2. Partnerships
3. Professional development
4. Accountability and evaluation systems
5. College and career readiness standards
6. Course sequences
7. Credit transfer agreements
8. Guidance counseling and academic advisement
9. Teaching and learning strategies
10. Technical skills assessments

To evaluate these essential components, the NASDCTEc recommends that evaluation be aligned with the Data Quality Campaign (2009) that calls for matching student-level education and employment records to gather valid and reliable data on student outcomes. The NADSCTEc also emphasizes "timely data to evaluate and improve the effectiveness of POS" (n.d., p. 3). These recommendations represent good progress; however, nowhere in them is there a suggestion that program evaluation should pay attention to issues of equitable outcomes for student subgroups. The document is silent on issues pertaining to outcomes and equity gaps that may be revealed if data are disaggregated. Without student subgroup analysis it is nearly impossible to create an accurate picture of program performance overall or at the student subgroup level. What happens to diverse student groups should be an essential element of any evaluation of career pathways and programs of study.

A recent report on Perkins IV by Klein et al. (2014) reveals the current status of CTE education in the United States, including the implementation of programs of study aligned with career clusters and career pathways. Pointing to a lack of specificity in financing, implementation, and evaluation of CTE, Klein and his colleagues offered the discouraging finding that the implementation of programs of study (POS) is so diffuse and unregulated under Perkins IV that it is nearly impossible to paint a clear picture of what has happened with federal funding since 2006. With respect to

NEW DIRECTIONS FOR COMMUNITY COLLEGES • DOI: 10.1002/cc

evaluation of student participation and outcomes, Klein et al. observed, "Lack of clear definitions on what constitutes a POS student and the absence of standardized reporting requirements related to POS further confound state implementation efforts. To date, relatively few state or local Perkins subgrantees are capable of providing accurate counts of the students who participate in POS or their outcomes" (pp. 233–234). This report suggests it is virtually impossible to know who participates in POS and to determine how students benefit from these programs. Recommendations of Klein et al. focus on improving program evaluation, although they fall short of specifying evaluation methods that enable states and local entities to assess whether outcomes are distributed equitably among student subgroups.

Also recently released, the Center for Law and Social Policy (CLASP; 2014) developed the Alliance for Quality Career Pathway (AQCP) Framework to assist states and local/regional entities to measure career pathway performance. Whereas career pathways are not synonymous with CTE, the focus on career preparation is sufficiently similar to suggest the CLASP Framework has relevance to the evaluation of CTE (Bragg, 2012). The AQCP Framework recommends a set of state, local/regional, and participant measures to evaluate the career-pathway trajectories of students by specifying criteria and indicators for state and local/regional systems, as well as participants. Though this model does not require that student outcomes be assessed at the subgroup level, it takes a modest step in this direction by stating that one of the goals of the framework is to "reduce racial and ethnic disparities" (p. 5). To its credit, this framework goes farther than any others to suggest that evaluating programs should contribute to closing equity gaps.

CTE Program Review

Attempting to understand state program approval and program review pertaining to CTE after passage of Perkins IV, Merkley and Johnston (2007) conducted a study of these state-level processes. Their study documented postsecondary CTE program outcomes required by Perkins IV, and they also identified inadequacies. For example, their study showed a lack of ability of state agencies to evaluate student achievement based on recognized industry standards and a limited capacity to measure job placement into high-skill, high-demand occupations. Their study also raised awareness of the federal government's intension to raise the stakes on state agencies with authority to distribute federal dollars to local providers, including community colleges, documenting the challenges that states face under Perkins IV. Their study also raised questions about how new industry standards would be incorporated into program approval processes, how states would improve alignment between programs and employment, and how connections between secondary and postsecondary would be solidified.

Moreover, Merkley and Johnston documented CTE program review processes in 42 of the 50 states, noting that the frequency by which CTE programs required program review varied widely, from 1 to 10 years, with 4 years being the most typical time period. The indicators of program quality used by the states also varied widely but focused primarily on enrollment rates, graduation and completion rates, job placement rates, and program costs. They reported no evidence that state program review policies required or encouraged the disaggregation of outcomes by student subgroups, including special population groups. Thus, the state-endorsed program review policies focused on overall program performance, masking potential equity gaps in access, achievement, or outcomes between student subgroups.

These results provide an interesting yet troubling backdrop to recent findings of Klein et al. (2014) that point to little change to the national picture of CTE from the previous NAVE report (Silverberg et al., 2004). Klein et al. state, "With few exceptions, study analyses reproduced findings from the 2004 National Assessment of Vocational Education [NAVE] Final Report to Congress"(p. xxi). Finding lessened spending power due to inflation during the time Perkins IV was in effect, Klein et al. report reduced federal support for state and local programs that has resulted in diminished capacity for CTE. This finding, along with greater state discretion on the distribution of Perkins IV funds, may have lessened the impact of CTE programs overall.

To this point, there is surprisingly little description in Perkins IV and state policy about what program improvement means or how to do it relative to CTE. Among the vast array of evaluation methods presently used to measure and account for program quality, Levandowski (2014) argues that program review can be a useful tool for state boards, administrators, and trustees to apply to any program. Focusing his research on community colleges, Levandowski echoed an observation made more than 25 years ago by Glenny and Schmidtlein (1983) who argued there are few areas of state government that are more controversial but potentially more important than program review. When this function is used to provide objective assessments of the conditions under which students learn, program review is very useful. Levandowski states, "Program review, when properly used, offers [state and local] decision-makers a tool for assessing the quality of community college programs and services" (2014, p. 2). Whether focused on CTE or other instructional programs, program review can help practitioners make decisions about program improvement by ensuring that results are regularly and routinely considered in campus and unit planning, decision making, and budgeting. His conception of program review endorses responsive, timely, and ongoing data collection for the purposes of improving any program that a community college offers. Knowing how all students are performing is a critical element of his formula for a successful program review.

NEW DIRECTIONS FOR COMMUNITY COLLEGES • DOI: 10.1002/cc

Program Improvement in Illinois

Beginning in 2009, the Illinois Community College Board (ICCB) and the University of Illinois at Urbana-Champaign's Office of Community College Research and Leadership (OCCRL) partnered to create a program evaluation and continuous improvement process for career pathways and programs of study called Pathways to Results (PTR; Bragg & Bennett, 2012). Consistent with the state's guiding principles for implementation and evaluation of programs of study (see Taylor et al., 2009), PTR emerged as the community college system's preferred approach to program improvement. Using Perkins IV leadership funding, PTR was initially directed at programs of study but has expanded to include career pathways, adult and workforce education, and transfer education in a range of fields, including STEM.

Guiding principles for career pathways and programs of study provide a valuable way of framing implementation of the PTR process. The guiding principles seek practitioners to engage in (a) transformative leadership, with input from collaborative partners; (b) student access and engagement in programs and services; (c) alignment among education and training partners that facilitate student transition and transfer; (d) rigorous comprehensive curriculum, pedagogy, and career development that empower student learning, completion, and credential attainment; (e) professional development for instructional and administrative personnel to enhance student success; and (f) accountability and continuous program improvement to achieve equitable student education and employment outcomes.

Building on these guiding principles, PTR requires the commitment of individuals and groups, including partners, their team members, and students, who seek to ensure the success of all students by empowering their success and removing roadblocks that get in the way of their goal attainment (Bragg, McCambly, & Durham, 2016). Using student-level data to identify equity gaps in outcomes between racial, gender, low-income, and other underserved student groups, programs, along with processes and policies associated with those programs, are assessed to identify problems that impede the success of student groups. By gathering disaggregated data, concerns are defined, root causes are identified and analyzed, and plans are made to test solutions. To avoid focusing on deficits, exemplary cases are also identified and used as models to evaluate and spread improvements to other programs. In so doing, PTR provides a methodology to ensure that programs that produce equitable student outcomes are scaled to others.

Five critical processes for improving career pathways and programs of study are the focus of PTR, starting with (a) engagement and commitment of practitioners and partners, and continuing with (b) equity and outcomes assessment, (c) process assessment, (d) process improvement and evaluation, and (e) review and reflection. A brief description of these processes appears in Table 5.1. These processes are ordered in a way that makes sense for many PTR projects, but this order should be modified to fit local

Table 5.1   Pathways to Results Processes and Steps

Process	Steps
Engagement and Commitment	Engage leaders and form the partnership. Gather input from the partnership. Identify and convene the PTR team. Solidify the focus of the PTR improvement project using the charter.
Outcomes and Equity Assessment	Identify and select outcomes data and develop an understanding of equity. Engage institutional research staff in collecting and sharing data with the team. Review disaggregated student subgroup data from an equity perspective.
Process Assessment	Identify major processes (e.g., recruitment, assessment, instruction, advising, placement) that support student movement along a pathway and success in a program of study. Explain processes the team has selected for review, with a list of potential contributing factors to student subgroup results. Determine underlying reasons for problems, successes, and contributing factors.
Process Improvement and Evaluation	Identify solutions, also called process changes, and reach consensus on their implementation. Develop an implementation plan that includes a statement of goals, intended outcomes, roles and responsibilities, steps, timeline, cost, and resources. Develop an evaluation plan that includes goals, methods, and performance measures to evaluate the success of identified solutions.
Review and Reflection	Reflect individually on the PTR process by writing a brief reflective story about a significant idea, experience, or other aspect of the process. Meet as a group to reflect on what has been learned collectively about program improvement and student success. Come together create a group reflection that focuses on what can be sustained and scaled to other pathways and programs of study.

problems and needs. It is important for teams to jump into PTR at the point that makes sense for them, often either with the engagement and commitment process or outcomes and equity assessment. Where teams start may depend on the extent to which partners have been already engaged, or the extent to which student-level data are readily attainable to analyze student- and program-level performance.

The five PTR processes empower a team of practitioners and their partners to make meaningful improvements to programs, beginning with

Engagement and Commitment. This process focuses on engendering the involvement and support of individuals and organizations that are in the position (often also possessing the power and inclination) to facilitate program improvement. Believing that student success is facilitated by a broad-based, stakeholder approach, PTR requires the formation of a coalition of practitioners, including community college and other educators (e.g., Kindergarten through grade 12, adult, university), as well as students, employers, community leaders, and other stakeholders who understand that pathways to success are needed for all students.

Equity and outcomes assessment focuses on the systematic examination of disaggregated student data to identify problems with or barriers to programs that have the potential to serve student subgroups. This aspect of PTR is characterized by encouraging practitioners to be equity-minded in their examining of outcomes results (Dowd & Bensimon, 2014). As equity-minded practitioners, individuals recognize "deficit thinking" in the following passage from the PTR module on process assessment: "if we had better students, we would have better outcomes" (Harmon, Liss, & Umbricht, 2012, p. 3). As Harmon et al. note, the equity mindset that is encouraged by PTR asks practitioners to understand, "if we create better processes, our students will demonstrate better outcomes" (p. 3). This asset perspective turns deficit thinking on its head and dispels the notion that only some students are destined for success.

Process assessment allows PTR teams to investigate and document the nuanced processes that are integral to understanding how pathways and programs of study function. Using process mapping, practitioners determine how and why they fall short in enabling all student groups to achieve success. Process mapping points out gaps and inadequacies that impede student performance. Similarly, process mapping is used to document successful processes, identifying promising practices for adoption by other pathways and programs of study.

Process improvement and evaluation set into motion plans to implement, evaluate, and improve pathways and programs of study on a continuous basis. This phase of PTR is often already familiar to practitioners who are comfortable with planning new programs and excited to make changes. What is different here is that the decisions that practitioners make are grounded in data that guide their plans to reduce inequities between student subgroups, thereby raising performance for all learners. Changes that are made are not focused on what practitioners think might help but on evidence that shows how all students are performing.

Storytelling is a means of engaging practitioners in reflecting on what they are doing to improve programs and to support equitable student outcomes. Using the theory of double-loop learning (Argyris, 1993), PTR encourages storytelling that engenders deep understanding of what is working for diverse learners who are represented in pathways and programs of study. Discussion among practitioners who hold diverse perspectives, including the stereotypes and biases that are ever-present in human sense-making, helps practitioners to "new ways of thinking about their students, which impacts the ways they carry out their everyday practice.".

After 6 years, PTR has been implemented in 46 of the 48 community colleges in Illinois, with over 80 projects completed or in process. PTR has also been extended to other community colleges in the United States that are recipients of Trade Adjustment Act Community College and Career Training Act (TAACCCT) grant funds wherein PTR is part of a comprehensive, mixed-method evaluation that includes performance, implementation, and impact evaluation. Also in Illinois, PTR is extending into the ICCB's program review process, including review of CTE and transfer education programs.

The program review system of the ICCB (2008) represents a major way to support campus-level planning and decision making and ensures the continuing need, improved quality, and cost-effectiveness of instructional programs. During 2014–15, the ICCB offered small grants to community colleges to integrate PTR into the program review process. Several colleges took the state's offer, building an earlier PTR project completed at Lincolnland Community College (personal communications with Wendy Howerter, 2014). In response to the call for proposals, Illinois Central College is integrating PTR into program review. According to this college's proposal, the PTR process is expected "bring in more partners, additional data, more perspectives examining the problems, additional tools and resources, and an overall strategy that will lead to action steps and improvements that could be addressed before the end of the year" (Dietrich & Sutton, 2014, p. 4). Through this project and others like it, the ICCB, in partnership with OCCRL, will formalize guidance for community colleges that seeks to use PTR in conjunction with program review. As a result of these efforts, Illinois' integration of program improvement and program review offer a valuable way to integrate equity and outcomes assessment into the core mission of the community college. Coming full circle, program review will be driven by outcomes and equity assessment that are necessary for program improvement to become a reality.

Implementations for the Future

Reflecting on past efforts to use PTR to bring about program improvement rooted in the examination of equitable outcomes, there are some important lessons for practitioners. First, CTE and STEM education program evaluation require thoughtful implementation and careful scrutiny. Past policies and practices that complicate or diminish the capacity of states and localities to implementation program evaluation dedicated to improving pathways and programs of study need to be understood. Second, the necessity to gather student-level data that enables disaggregation of outcomes by student subgroups should be part of all continuous improvement, program review, and accountability efforts. It is essential to understand whether outcomes are distributed equitably to diverse student groups, and to do otherwise makes no sense. Recognition that federal Perkins legislation has identified some student groups as "special populations" but neglected other groups, including racial and ethnic minorities, represents a problem for program evaluation. Third, the role that practitioners play in outcomes and equity work is critical if program improvement is to be impactful. It is advantageous to involve researchers and evaluators in program evaluation, but it is equally or possibly even more important to include practitioners in continuous program improvement processes such as PTR. This on-the-ground work is essential if pathways and programs in CTE and STEM are going to fulfill the needs of all of the nation's diverse learners.

References

Argyris, C. (1993) *On organizational learning.* Cambridge, MA: Blackwell

Bragg, D. (2012). *Career and technical education.* In J., Levin & S., Kater (Eds), Understanding community colleges (pp. 187–202). London, England: Routledge/Taylor Francis

Bragg, D., & Bennett, S. (2012). *Introduction to Pathways to Results* (rev. ed.). Champaign, IL: Office of Community College Research and Leadership, University of Illinois at Urbana-Champaign. Retrieved from http://occrl.illinois.edu/docs/librariesprovider4/ptr/ptr-intro-module.pdf?sfvrsn=13

Bragg, D., McCambly, H., & Durham, B. (2016). Catching the spark: Student activism and student data as a catalyst for systemic transformation. *Change, The Magazine of Higher Learning, 48*(3), 36–47.

Center for Law and Social Policy. (2014). *Shared vision, Strong systems: The Alliance for Quality Career Pathways Framework Version 1.0.* Washington, DC: Author. Retrieved from http://www.clasp.org/resources-and-publications/files/aqcp-framework-version-1-0/AQCP-Framework.pdf

Data Quality Campaign. (2009). *The next step: Using longitudinal data systems to improve student success.* Retrieved from http://dataqualitycampaign.org/resource/next-step-using-longitudinal-data-systems-improve-student-success/

Dietrich, J., & Sutton, K. (2014). *FY 2015 program of study local implementation grant.* Springfield, IL: Illinois Community College Board.

Dowd, A., & Bensimon, E. (2014). *Engaging the race question: Accountability and equity in U.S. higher education.* New York, NY: Teachers College Press.

Glenny, L. A., & Frank A., Schmidtlein (1983). The role of the state in the governance of higher education. *Educational Evaluation and Policy Analysis, 5*(2), 113–153.

Harmon, T., Liss, L., & Umbricht, M. (2012). *Phase three: Process assessment.* Champaign, IL: Office of Community College Research and Leadership, University of Illinois at Urbana-Champaign.

Illinois Community College Board. (2008). *Illinois Community College System program review statewide summary.* Springfield, IL: Author. Retrieved from https://www.iccb.org/iccb/wp-content/pdfs/manuals/program_review/ICCB_Program_Review_2017-2021.pdf

Klein, S., Sheil, A. R., White, R., Staklis, S., Alfeld, C., Dailey, C. R., et al. (2014). *Evaluation of the implementation of the Carl D. Perkins Career and Technical Education Act of 2006: Finance, accountability, and programs of study.* Research Triangle Park, NC: RTI International.

Kotamraju, P. (2010). A new direction for CTE accountability and evaluation. *Techniques, 85*(3), 50–53.

Levandowski, A. (2014). *How evaluation practice, knowledge construction, value, and social programming predict utilization of program review recommendations by community college department chairs* (Unpublished doctoral dissertation). University of Illinois at Urbana-Champaign, Urbana, Illinois.

McCambly, H., Rodriguez, J., & Bragg, D. (2016). *Process and practice assessment* (rev. ed.). Champaign, IL: Office of Community College Research and Leadership, University of Illinois at Urbana-Champaign. Retrieved from http://occrl. illinois.edu/docs/librariesprovider4/ptr/process-assessment.pdf?sfvrsn=16

Merkley, R., & Johnston, G. (2007). *State approval policies and procedures for postsecondary career and technical education.* St. Paul, MN: National Center for Career and Technical Education, University of Minnesota. Retrieved from http://www.nrccte. org/sites/default/files/publication-files/state_approval_policies-cc.pdf

Silverberg, W., Warner, E., Fong, M., & Goodwin, D. (2004). *National Assessment of Vocational Education: Final Report to Congress: Executive Summary.* Washington, DC: U.S. Department of Education, Office of the Under Secretary, Policy and Program Studies Service.

Taylor, J. L., Kirby, C. L., Bragg, D. D., Oertle, K. M., Jankowski, N. A., & Khan, S. S. (2009, July). *Illinois programs of study guide.* Champaign, IL: University of Illinois, Office of Community College Research and Leadership. Retrieved from http:// occrl.illinois.edu/files/Projects/pos/POSguide.pdf

DEBRA D. BRAGG *is the Director of Community College Research Initiatives at the University of Washington Seattle.*

6

This chapter reviews the literature, gender and CTE, classroom climate, and faculty–student interactions and presents results of a qualitative study on gender microaggressions in community college CTE classrooms.

Unwelcoming Classroom Climates: The Role of Gender Microaggressions in CTE

Jaime Lester, Brice Struthers, Aoi Yamanaka

Career and technical education (CTE) programs at the community college have a significant history. Arguably beginning with the passage of the Vocational Education Act of 1963, vocational education, as a precursor to CTE, has remained a prominent aspect of the mission of U.S. community colleges. The number of students in CTE in community colleges is substantial. According to the National Center for Education Statistics (NCES), in 2004–2005, more than 2,000 U.S. 2-year institutions awarded a postsecondary credential in one or more CTE fields of study (Levesque et al., 2008). During the same year, 64% of students seeking associate degrees and 81% of students in certificate programs majored in occupational fields (Levesque et al.). Occupational programs, which are typically certificate granting and noncredit, often serve as gateway programs into CTE accounting for an additional 5 million individuals in fall 2008, representing 40% of community college student enrollment (Levesque et al.).

Although women tend to dominate CTE enrollments, they remain concentrated into historically feminized fields; the U.S. Department of Labor defines nontraditional occupations for females as those where females make up less than 25% of workers. The U.S. Department of Labor found that in 2012, women made up less than 2% of electricians, automotive service technicians, and less than 5% of welders (U.S. Department of Labor, 2012). A recent report by American Association for University Women (St. Rose & Hill, 2013) states, "Men were more likely than women to earn certificates as welders, electricians, and heating/AC/ventilation (HVAC) and automotive technicians—jobs that offer much higher wages than those popular among

NEW DIRECTIONS FOR COMMUNITY COLLEGES, no. 178, Summer 2017 © 2017 Wiley Periodicals, Inc.
Published online in Wiley Online Library (wileyonlinelibrary.com) • DOI: 10.1002/cc.20254

women (with the exception of health care jobs)" (p. 15). Those feminized fields tend to have lower earning potential with fewer opportunities as pathways to higher paying STEM fields, such as computer science. Reasons for the isolation of women in specific fields is largely unknown with some pertinent research found in science, technology, engineering, and mathematics (STEM) literature. Most prominently, research identifies that female students in CTE courses experience highly masculine subcultures, differential teacher bias, a lack of role models, and curriculum that focuses on competition rather than collaborative interaction (Lester, 2008, 2010; Trusty, 2002).

The purpose of this chapter is to further the research and discourse on women in CTE by presenting the theory of gender microaggressions as an explanatory framework of why women continue to opt out of CTE or remain concentrated in feminized fields. We argue, and present vignettes of individual classrooms, that microinvalidations, as a form of microaggressions, are present in pedagogy and peer interactions thus creating unfriendly climates for women students. The chapter concludes with concrete and practical suggestions of how to examine and address gender microaggressions in CTE with implications for STEM fields as well.

Theoretical Framework

Microaggression research began in the 1970s and has more recently expanded into new areas including the higher education sector. Microaggressions are subtle insults that are commonly directed to an individual who is believed to associate with a particular group (Sue et al., 2007). Sue (2010), among others considered leaders in the research of microaggressions, found that there are several types of microaggressive behaviors including microinsult, microassault, and microinvalidations (Sue et al., 2007). A microinsult consists of environmental and interpersonal interactions that express the stereotypes of another group and typically are unconscious (Sue et al., 2007). Microassaults are conscious degrading verbal or nonverbal actions that hurt an individual of another group (Sue et al., 2007). Microinvalidations cue individuals to feel negated or neglected from their experiential reality (Sue et al., 2007).

Each subcategory may apply to a particular group and in recent research, Nadal (2013) has looked more specifically at how microaggressions apply to gender. A chapter in Nadal's book focuses on revealing a set number of themes around gender microaggressions, which include sexual objectification, assumption of inferiority, assumption of traditional gender roles, use of sexist language, denial of individual sexism, invisibility, denial of the reality of sexism, and environmental gender microaggressions. Each theme presented relates to one or several subcategories of microaggressions and helps to provide a framework of the current study on gender microaggressions.

NEW DIRECTIONS FOR COMMUNITY COLLEGES • DOI: 10.1002/cc

In addition to the knowledge on gender microaggressions, researchers have looked at the impact of the microaggression in the classroom. Much of the research on classroom microaggressions focuses on racial rather than gender-oriented microaggressive acts. However, the studies on racial microaggressions in the classroom reveal the unfavorable effect microaggressions have on students (Boysen, 2009, 2012; Solorzano, Ceja, & Yosso, 2000). The researchers, in their most recent study, found that females experience a variety of microaggressive behaviors in the classroom and are more satisfied with teachers who actively address, rather than ignore, microaggressive acts in the classroom. The results reveal the complex nature of how microaggressions are expressed in a classroom environment.

Women in CTE

The dearth of literature on gender in CTE necessitates a review of literature as it relates to STEM fields. Research identifies learning styles, interactions with teachers, and perceived social support as influences on female student success connected to classroom-based experiences. Philbin, Meier, Huffman, & Boverie (1995) found that female students in information science courses tend to fail because of an "invisible barrier" between the student and instructor. Female students felt disconnected from the learning environment because of the instructor's authoritative learning style. A recent study from Wasburn and Miller (2004–2005) noted that, in nontraditional female technology classrooms, females received differential treatment compared to males. In the same study, Wasburn and Miller found 20% of the female students did not feel comfortable asking questions in class and a third of the female students did not have confidence in their technology skills.

An additional concern found in research is with pedagogical design and styles (Heffler, 2001; Tindall & Hamil, 2003). According to Kember and McNaught (2007), effective teaching consists in part of (a) teaching and curriculum designs that focus on developing students' skills of critical thinking, teamwork, and communication; (b) integration of a variety of learning tasks that engage students, such as discussion and group work, in order for meaningful learning to take place; (c) establishment of legitimate and sympathetic relationships with students to enhance interactions; and (d) enhancement of students' motivations by showing teachers' own enthusiasm and providing interesting and active classes. The previous research indicates that positive interactions with classmates are beneficial to female students in computer science classes because the interactions develop female students' stronger sense of community and belonging in their academic department or classroom (Parviainen, 2008). Female students tend to desire instructors who facilitate learning by connecting material to practical application and more collaborative work with classmates because they create more opportunities for interactions among classmates

NEW DIRECTIONS FOR COMMUNITY COLLEGES • DOI: 10.1002/cc

(Barrett, 2006; Parviainen, 2008; Philbin et al., 1995; Seymour & Hewitt, 1997).

Male students in the studies identified more with an authoritative instructor who assumed an expert role (Barrett, 2006; Philbin et al., 1995). When pedagogical methods suitable for men are assumed as appropriate for females, gender deficits can be problematic (Philbin et al., 1995). McCarthy (2009) found that females "remembered awkward situations in technology education courses that were the result of thoughtless jokes or comments by teachers as well as male students" (p. 18). Using male pronouns, calling on male students, and using male examples all have an effect on the perceived acceptance of females in STEM classrooms. The climate of classrooms and labs makes female students feel included or unwanted (McCarthy, 2009). Additionally, female faculty underrepresentation in nontraditional programs illustrates to female students that the discipline attracts few female candidates (Blickenstaff, 2005).

Experiences of Women in STEM

An ethnographic case study was applied to examine microaggressions against female students in typically male-dominated career and technical education courses at a mid-Atlantic community college composed of several campuses. A case study is "chosen precisely because researchers are interested in insight, discovery, and interpretation rather than hypothesis testing" (Merriam, 1988, p. 10). In addition, it is most applicable "when the focus is on a contemporary phenomenon within some real-life context" (Yin, 2003, p. 1). An ethnographic case study provides in-depth descriptions of the culture being studied and allows members to tell their stories (Van Maanen, 1988). Because the definitions and identifications of gender are culturally and contextually specific, this research design assisted in uncovering the individual ways in which individual students experience gender microaggressions within classroom settings.

The data collection consisted of observations of 26 individual course meetings from 5 CTE courses at the community college and 9 interviews. The research was conducted in the Spring and Summer semesters. To select the courses the researchers used the CTE categories of mechanic and repair technologies, preengineering, and construction trades in the community college course catalog. The courses were selected based on their low numbers of female representation (and in collaboration with the study site). The researchers contacted the individual faculty via e-mail and used the snowball sampling method to identify additional courses to observe in the following academic semester. Individuals who worked in programs designed to recruit females in CTE in the community college also assisted in choosing courses and making contact with instructors. The community college approved our research and was aware of the recruitment of students. About 82 hours of observations were conducted across the courses. The purpose of the observations was to identify whether and how microaggressions occurred in the classrooms. The observations included both lecture and laboratory class formats. The observers (researchers) documented interpersonal interactions; the physical classroom space; representations of the field in posters, texts, and instructional aids (videos, manuals); and how students positioned themselves in seats and laboratory spaces in a wide range of class formats, such as lecture, group work, tests, and outside activities.

The researchers conducted nine interviews with female students. The purpose of the interviews was to exert as much information from the personal experiences of female students in CTE classrooms. All of the female students who were enrolled in the courses that the researchers observed were recruited in person and asked to participate. All interviews were professionally transcribed and lasted approximately 1 hour. The interview questions were compiled based on two previous surveys, the Microaggressions Against Women Scale (MAWS) and the Racial and Ethnic Microaggressions Scale (REMS; Nadal, 2011; Owen, Tao, & Rodolfa, 2010). The MAWS is designed to measure different forms of microaggressions against females during the therapy process by examining the 15 specific, common microaggressions (Owen et al., 2010). The REMS is used to measure the influence of racial and ethnic microaggressions by assessing the frequency of specific microaggression situations over the past 6 months (Nadal, 2011). Based on these scales, the researchers developed open-ended interview questions that included the experiences of the female students in the classroom, a rationale for the seating locations that female students chose, female students' perceptions of the classroom climate, and their interactions with peers and instructors.

The primary methods of data analysis of this research were the systematic coding of interview transcripts and observation notes in order to develop thematic patterns. Codes were developed from the literature and transcripts using a constant comparative method that identified and generalized patterns of the females' interactions with male students and with instructors, recorded the female students' experience of microaggressions, and gathered other information, such the type of learning environment.

Vignettes of CTE Classrooms

The findings from this study identify three areas of microinvalidations: (a) a consistent pattern of female isolation across all of the CTE courses, (b) traditional lecture pedagogy that led to little interaction and a competitive classroom climate, and (c) gendered language that differentiated male and female students. We present these findings in two composite vignettes to illustrate the presence and impact of microinvalidations.

Instructional Technology and Pedagogy. The instructor stands at the front of the classroom with a single page torn out from the course textbook. He reads from the page directing students to the same page in their book, chapter 4. The students sit at computers with a seat between each of them, a practice used to separate the students during the beginning classroom computer-based quiz. He asks the students if they have any questions about chapter 3, the chapter covered in the previous course meeting. Several students ask questions and the instructor writes them on the Smartboard located at the front of the room. The lecture continues with strict attention to the wording used in the textbook, examples of coding up on the Smartboard and students attempting the work on their individual computers. Half the students are reading e-mail or browsing on the Internet. Two students begin to discuss concepts used in Java programming attempting to help one another. The instructor reacts stating, "I know you are talking about the class but when you do you may be missing something. Let's agree to pay attention to lecture. I'll give you time for discussion." No time for discussion is given at the end of class this course meeting or subsequently. The class takes a short break and the only female student sits alone eating a snack outside the classroom while the male students socialize and collaborate on homework.

As class was coming to a close, the content of the lecture turns to Boolean r in computer coding. The instructor states, "If one male and one female come to the door for class, according to Boolean r, one is true and one is false. They are mutually exclusive. Say two males show up, that would be both false. Say two females show up, that would be false. This is to say you need two that are mutually exclusive." He continues, "Remember what I told you if two males come to the door of the classroom, only males would be allowed. If two girls came first, only girls would be allowed in classroom." The students all nod in agreement seemingly unsurprised by the use of gender to describe a concept in computer science.

Construction Technologies and Peer Interaction

Outside of a classroom building near a large shedlike structure, two groups of students work on building structures. One group consists of four women who are collaborating on an enclosure for the HVAC for the main classroom building. Another all-male group is digging a series of holes to build a foundation near the shedlike building. About 50 yards from each other, the two groups dramatically differ in how they interact among themselves and with the instructor. The female group is constantly in conversation discussing their processes: what tool to use or the appropriate nail. Their work is steady, correct, and collaborative. The instructor walks between the two groups reviewing their work and, at times, adding suggestions or critique. The instructor spends 50% more time with the female group often asserting his expertise while just silently reviewing the work of the all-male group. The male group of about four people works in spurts with at least one male hanging around and not actively participating. Their discussion, although frequent, is not focused on the work; often they joke around using inappropriate slang, with ease.

Around 10 a.m., an hour into the 6-hour class meeting, one of the male students comes over to work with the women. A female student begins to ask him a question and he fails to respond. She asks him another question and he grunts, barely acknowledging her presence. She gives up and goes back to working with the women and the male student continues constructing the roof for the HVAC enclosure. This type of interaction is common in the all-female group when a male comes to assist.

A few hours later, more wood is needed for their HVAC structure. A female student makes a remark about going to get wood from the shed. The instructor immediately steps in noting that she does not have the physical strength to carry the wood. During another one of the class periods, one male student told a female student that she would not have enough physical strength to carry the water hose before she even attempted to do so. The physical abilities of the female students were regularly called into question despite the fact they seemed willing to perform these tasks.

In the two vignettes, similar dynamics existed resulting from the instructor pedagogy, the physical structure of the classroom, and gender bias that led to subtle insults or demeaning comments. Although instructors used a variety of teaching practices and pedagogy, the majority tended to focus more on lectures and individual learning as opposed to more collaborative styles. In one-way lecture classes, there were limited discussions or collaborative group work and students did not have opportunities to interact with other students. The classroom settings were a contributing factor in students' interactions. In this study, the computer science classes were held in computer labs in which unmovable individual desks and chairs were arranged in several rows and computer screens created distance between students and instructors and between students. Therefore, the computer lab classrooms were not designed to enhance interaction among students; rather they created isolation between students. The construction technologies class was not in a traditional classroom but had two different building projects that bifurcated the students into two gendered groups with little interaction across those groups. Finally, instructors used gender-laden language to illustrate concepts; this signaled a differentiation between genders. In a computer science course, the instructor was illustrating the point of the Boolean r in computer coding. The instructor gives the example of gender to illustrate parity in true or false statements. He used the word "girls" instead of "women" for a female case while using the word "men" for a male case and the description of the male's case preceded the female's. In a construction technologies course, the instructor tended to spend the majority of his time with the all-female group working to build a fence around a HVAC unit on the college campus. Spending more time with the female group signaled that the females were less able to build a structure and, in fact, comments were made to that effect. The result of these practices, intentional or not, is to create environments that are unwelcoming to women.

NEW DIRECTIONS FOR COMMUNITY COLLEGES • DOI: 10.1002/cc

Implications for Practice

The findings in this study have several practical implications worth noting that concern faculty professional development, pedagogy, and classroom management. As to not place the full onus of responsibility on faculty, community colleges need to consider new practices that support faculty development as more diverse student populations enroll in courses. As recruitment practices formally through community colleges as well as movements to support more women and historically underrepresented groups in STEM fields, faculty need additional support to review and alter their practices to continue to encourage and support those new and continuing students. This section outlines several potential new practices for community colleges.

Pedagogy Discussion and Professional Development.   The findings in this study have several practical implications worth noting. First, community colleges need to consider additional professional development for faculty teaching practices. As noted, the instructors rarely used active learning strategies that are found to have a clear positive impact on student learning. And, as we illustrate in this study, these strategies have the potential to increase peer interaction and challenge implicit bias of female students abilities, both physical and intellectual, in CTE. The use of problem-based and experiential learning is well documented as having a positive impact on student learning and is the focus of many STEM fields. Networks such as SENCER, POGIL, BioQuest, and Project Kaleidoscope offer a variety of workshops, conferences, and teaching materials with some that are specific to the community college setting. Other materials are readily adaptable to different disciplines and contexts. Moreover, community colleges can leverage their investment in teaching and the collective teaching knowledge on their campuses to support pedagogy-related discussions in the form of book clubs, speakers, and training to further the use of active learning pedagogy. Again, the potential benefit is beyond increasing women in CTE.

Implicit Bias Workshops.   Second and related to the first point, more conversation is needed with instructors to directly challenge implicit gender bias. Although we conclude that instructors do not intentionally emphasize gender differences, the use of gender language, attention to male students, and classroom climate could have a positive impact on female student success. Implicit bias workshops are becoming more common related to microaggressions, work–life issues, and STEM education. For example, The Ohio State University offers training, performances, and conversations to surface gender-related bias. These programs are easily tailored to a community college population and for teaching practices. University of California–Davis also required implicit bias training for hiring committees with a well-designed website full of informational resources. See http://ucd-advance.ucdavis.edu/implicit-bias

Programs and Partnership for Women in CTE.   A third area for consideration to increase the number of women in CTE is partnerships with vocational programs in high schools and recruitment in local industry. Although not presented in detail in this chapter, women in CTE classrooms appeared to benefit from having other women to collaborate and socialize with inside or outside of class. Often formed as study groups, the women tended to sit together in class and support their academic work, as they are largely isolated from their male colleagues. Programs that more formally bring women in CTE together for mutual support could help to locate more women across student cohorts to create an even larger network. Women in CTE are a self-selected group; they self-select into CTE prior to enrollment in the community college. To increase the number of women enrolling in CTE, community colleges can reach out to high schools to publicize the value of CTE for women, especially those more traditionally male CTE areas. Similarly, community colleges should consider recruiting women in local industry who would benefit from a certificate or skill development. These individuals then become mentors and role models for younger women seeking jobs in the near future.

Conclusion

The number of women in CTE and STEM is a major concern as the United States seeks to increase educated workers in technical fields. Whereas the research in STEM points to some understanding of why women opt out of technical fields, little is known about CTE. Our study illuminates the impact of classroom climate including attitudes of instructors and peers and how community colleges can intervene to promote women in CTE. Changes in instructor awareness of implicit bias, instructor pedagogy, and creating or growing supportive programs for women in particular have significant potential to increase the number of women in CTE, STEM, and eventual earning potential.

References

Barrett, K. R. (2006). Gender and differences in online teaching styles. In E. M. Trauth (Ed.), *Encyclopedia of gender and information technology* (pp. 372–377). Hershey, PA: Idea Group Reference.

Blickenstaff, J. C. (2005). Females and science careers. *Gender and Education, 17*(2), 369–386.

Boysen, G. A. (2009). Bias in the classroom: Types, frequencies, and responses. *Teaching of Psychology, 36*, 12–17. doi: 10.1080/875675552012654831

Boysen, G. A. (2012). Teacher and student perceptions of microaggressions in college classrooms. *College Teaching, 60*(3), 122–129. doi: 10.1177/0098628312456626

Heffler, B. (2001). Individual learning style and the Learning Style Inventory. *Educational Studies, 27*(3), 307–316.

Kember, D., & McNaught, C. (2007). *Enhancing university teaching.* New York: Routledge.

Levesque, K., Laird, J., Hensley, E., Choy, S., Cataldi, E., & Hudson, L. (2008). *Career and technical education in the United States: 1900 to 2005* (NCES 2008-035). Washington, DC: National Center for Education Statistics. Retrieved from http://nces.ed.gov/pubs2008/2008035.pdf

Lester, J. (2008). Performing gender in the workplace: Gender socialization, power, and identity among females faculty. *Community College Review, 34*(4), 277–305.

Lester, J. (2010). Females in male-dominated career technical education programs at community colleges: Barriers to participation and success. *Journal of Females and Minorities in Science and Education, 16*(1), 51–66.

McCarthy, R. (2009, October). Beyond smash and crash: Gender-friendly tech ed. *Technology Teacher*, pp. 16–21.

Merriam, S. B. (1988). *Case study research in education: A qualitative approach.* San Francisco: Jossey-Bass.

Nadal, K. L. (2011). The Racial and Ethnic Microaggressions Scale (REMS): Construction, reliability, and validity. *Journal of Counseling Psychology, 58*(4), 470–480. https://doi.org/10.1037/a0025193

Nadal, K. L. (2013). A review of the microaggression literature. In *That's so gay! Microaggressions and the lesbian, gay, bisexual, and transgender community.* American Psychological Association.

Owen, J., Tao, K., & Rodolfa, E. (2010). Microaggressions and females in short-term psychotherapy: Initial evidence. *Counseling Psychologist, 38*(7), 923–946. doi: 10.1177/0011000010376093

Parviainen, M. L. (2008). The experiences of females in computer science: The importance of awareness and communication. *Human Architecture: Journal of the Sociology of Self-Knowledge, 6*(4), 87–94.

Philbin, M., Meier, E., Huffman, S., & Boverie, P. (1995). A survey of gender and learning styles. *Sex Roles, 32*(7/8), 485–494.

Seymour, E., & Hewitt, N. (1997). *Talking about leaving: Why undergraduates leave the sciences.* Boulder, CO: Westview Press.

Solórzano, D., Ceja, M., & Yosso, T. (2000). Critical race theory, racial microaggressions, and campus racial climate: The experiences of African American college students. *Journal of Negro Education, 69*(1/2), 60–73.

St. Rose, A., & Hill, C. (2013). *Women in community colleges: Access to success.* Washington, DC: American Association of University Women. Retrieved from http://www.aauw.org/files/2013/05/women-in-community-colleges.pdf

Sue, D. W. (2010). *Microaggressions in everyday life: Race, gender, and sexual orientation.* Hoboken, NJ: John Wiley & Sons.

Sue, D. W., Capodilupo, C. M., Torino, G. C., Bucceri, J. M., Holder, A. M. B., Nadal, K. L., & Esquilin, M. (2007). Racial microaggressions in everyday life: Implications for clinical practice. *American Psychologist, 62*(4), 271–286. https://doi.org/10.1037/0003-066X.62.4.271

Tindall, T., & Hamil, B. (2003). Gender disparity in science education: The causes, consequences, and solution. *Education, 125*(2), 282–295.

Trusty, J. (2002). Effects of high school course-taking and other variables on choice of science and mathematics college majors. *Journal of Counseling and Development, 80*(4), 464–474.

U.S. Department of Labor, (2012). *Occupational outlook handbook, 2012–13 edition.* Washington, DC: Author. Retrieved from http://www.bls.gov/ooh/construction-and-extraction/electricians.htm

Van Maanen, J. (1988). *Tales of the field: On writing ethnography.* Chicago: University of Chicago Press.

Wasburn, M. H., & Miller, S. G. (2004–2005). Retaining undergraduate women in science, engineering, and technology: A survey of a student organization. *Journal of College Student Retention, 6*(2), 155–168.

Yin, R. K. (2003). *Case study research, design and methods* (3rd ed., vol. 5). Thousand Oaks, CA: Sage.

JAIME LESTER is an associate professor of higher education at George Mason University.

BRICE STRUTHERS is an associate academic innovation specialist at American Council on Education.

AOI YAMANAKA is a doctoral student and instructor at George Mason University.

NEW DIRECTIONS FOR COMMUNITY COLLEGES • DOI: 10.1002/cc

7

This chapter examines exemplary practices and challenges of recruiting and retaining women in information technology programs in an Iowa community college context.

Recruiting and Retaining Women in Information Technology Programs

Practices and Challenges in Iowa Community Colleges

Yu (April) Chen, Arlene de la Mora, Mari Kemis

Why Are Women in Information Technology Important?

The computing profession is growing at a faster rate than other professions in the science, technology, engineering, and math (STEM) fields. According to the U.S. Department of Labor, there will be nearly 1.3 million computing-related job openings from 2010 to 2020 in the United States (Richards & Terkanian, 2013). The nation needs to satisfy this workforce growth by preparing sufficient and well-educated job candidates. However, the current college graduates majoring in computer sciences can fill less than 40% of the job openings. It is imperative to expand the pool of college students in computer sciences and information technology (IT), and most important, to recruit and retain more students who have been underrepresented in these fields.

Women are one of the underrepresented student groups in computer sciences and IT. Although numerous literatures highlighted women's achievements in college education (e.g., National Center for Women & Information Technology [NCWIT], 2014; National Science Foundation [NSF] & National Center for Science and Engineering Statistics [NCSES], 2015), women remain underrepresented in male-dominated majors such as computer sciences and IT. Women have earned more than half of all bachelor's degrees since the late 1990s (NSF & NCSES, 2015). Although the enrollment of women in computer science majors has increased considerably from 2002 to 2012, the proportion of women who earned a bachelor's degree in the same time frame has declined. (NSF & NCSES, 2015).

The gender imbalance in the fields of computer science and IT is also true in the workforce. Currently in the United States, women hold more

New Directions for Community Colleges, no. 178, Summer 2017 © 2017 Wiley Periodicals, Inc.
Published online in Wiley Online Library (wileyonlinelibrary.com) • DOI: 10.1002/cc.20255

than half (57%) of the professional jobs. However, only 26% of professional computing occupations are held by women. The representation of under-represented minority women is even less. In particular, African-American women make up 3% of the computing workforce. Asian-American women made up 5% and Hispanic women comprised only 2% of the computing workforce (NSF & NCSES, 2015); whereas the proportions of the under-represented minority women in the U.S. population are 12.8% for African-American women, 5.4% for Asian-American women, and 16.9% for Hispanic women (U.S. Census Bureau, 2014). Moreover, only a few women held a management-level position in the computing and IT area. Among the Fortune 500 companies, for example, only 4% of the chief executive officers, 14% of the executive officer positions, and 16% of board of directors positions were held by women (NCWIT, 2014).

Increasing the number of female graduates and workers in computer science and IT majors is not only an economic and social need. It is also desirable for the stability and quality of women's lives. For example, a highly competitive salary and less risk of unemployment are two of the advantages of the computing and IT professions. As mentioned previously, the computing and IT workforce has been projected to develop into 2020. In sum, the gap between the job market needs and gender imbalance should be filled by increasing the enrollment of female students in computer science and IT majors and eventually increasing the number of women in IT occupations.

Why Are Women Underrepresented in IT?

A variety of studies have been focusing on studying the barriers that keep women away from IT professions. A publication from the American Association of University Women (AAUW) cited research evidence to emphasize the impact of stereotypes and biases (Hill, Corbett, & St. Rose, 2010). For example, girls' performance in a challenging math test can be significantly lower when stereotypes against gender were presented (Spencer, Steele, & Quinn, 1999). STEM departments in higher education institutions should be cognizant of how environmental factors can contribute to women's success; and therefore, be dedicated to organizational changes to promote women's success in science and engineering (Hill et al., 2010).

Another way to study this issue is to investigate why some women choose to enter and successfully stay in the IT area. For example, Turner and colleagues (2002) conducted a survey of 275 women who were employed in IT careers in different countries. They found that school experiences (both high school and college) and influences from male family members, friends, and colleagues played important roles in respondents' career decisions.

Furthermore, Trauth (2002) and Trauth & Howcroft (2006) proposed the individual differences theory as an analytical framework of gender and IT. The individual differences theory views women as individuals with distinct personalities, socioeconomic backgrounds, and cultural experiences; therefore, they would react differently to the socially constructed IT concept. By analyzing women who successfully persisted in IT, researchers may identify individual and social factors that enable women to overcome systematic barriers and thus be successful in IT. In a multicountry comparative study, Trauth, Quesenberry, and Huang (2008) employed this individual differences framework to understand how cultural factors influence career choice of women in the global IT workforce. They identified several terms for identifying women's traditional roles such as child care, parental care, and working outside the home. The social and cultural factors that may moderate the influence of these perceptions on women's IT career choice include gender career norms, social class status, economic opportunity, and gender stereotypes about aptitude (Trauth et al., 2008).

In contrast to this study, Ahuja (2002) took a different route and directly identified the barriers preventing women's success in IT. Through a systematic literature review, Ahuja indicated that both social factors and structural factors may prevent women from choosing to enter and persist in the IT workforce. Specifically, social factors such as social expectation and work–family conflict will negatively influence career choice and persistence of women in IT. Structural factors such as occupational culture and lack of role models will play a critical role in keeping women away from IT professions (Ahuja).

Previous literature provides various frameworks to analyze the relationship between gender and IT careers. Future studies may use these frameworks for specific contexts. In particular, researchers and practitioners may learn from the literature and reveal strategies for recruiting and retaining women in IT within the community college context.

Community College's Role in Increasing Women in STEM

The community college has been playing a critical role in preparing female graduates in STEM fields. First, community college's transfer function provides a vital pathway for underprepared and underrepresented minority students (including females) to achieve bachelor's degrees and beyond in STEM fields. In the 2006–2007 academic year, 52.2% of science, engineering, and health graduates with bachelor's degrees attended community college during their education journey (Mooney & Foley, 2011). Women in STEM are more likely to start from community colleges (Tsapogas, 2004). Compared to males (42.8%), a greater proportion of female graduates (53.8%) have ever attended community college (Mooney & Foley, 2011).

On the other hand, the career and technical education (CTE) programs in community colleges have responded to the national needs of increasing the number of well-trained, competitive technology workers for the U.S. workforce. Within the fast-growing computing occupations, computer system design and related services drive the industry growth. According to the

NEW DIRECTIONS FOR COMMUNITY COLLEGES • DOI: 10.1002/cc

U.S. Department of Labor, the service industry accounted for just 20% of all jobs in computing occupations in 2010 but is projected to generate more than half of the new computing jobs between 2010 and 2020 (Lockard & Wolf, 2012). It is certain that the role of CTE programs in community colleges will be essential in meeting the future workforce needs.

Women have comprised approximately half of the CTE enrollment in community colleges; however, very few of them have enrolled in male-dominant areas such as IT (Bailey, Alfonso, Scott, & Leinbach, 2004; Lester, 2010). Based on a case study of female students enrolled in STEM CTE programs, Lester (2010) suggested that the lack of institutional support for enrolling in CTE programs and the gender bias in hypermasculine classrooms might hinder female students' success.

Previous studies on transfer, CTE programs, and women enrolled in male-dominant majors provided new directions and analytical tools for this study. Specifically, we are aiming at revealing the exemplary practices and challenges in terms of recruiting and retaining women in IT programs at community colleges. We interviewed IT program coordinators, faculty members, and academic counselors who work closely with female students in Iowa community colleges. Through analyzing interview transcripts, we identified exemplary practices that facilitated female students' success, as well as challenges that prevent community college educators from further helping women. We finally provided several recommendations for community college practitioners based on our analysis.

Women in IT Programs at Iowa Community Colleges

All 15 Iowa community colleges offer IT programs as credit CTE programs (Iowa Department of Education, 2014a). It is one of the most popular CTE programs offered by Iowa community colleges in 2014. During fiscal year 2012, more than 400 students earned an academic credential in IT programs across Iowa. This is about a 60% increase from fiscal year 2010 (Iowa Department of Education, 2014b). However, the gender imbalance still exists in most of the IT programs.

In this study, we conducted interviews with IT program coordinators, faculty members, and academic counselors at three Iowa community colleges. All three community colleges are considered large institutions with total enrollment ranging from 6,623 to 14,268 in the fall of 2014 (Iowa Department of Education, 2014c). All three community colleges have well-established IT programs and are aware of the underrepresentation of women in IT enrollment and retention.

Two of the interviews were conducted at a distance using either phone or conference call. The third one was conducted face to face. Two interviews were individual; the third one was a focus-group interview. All interviews were recorded and transcribed by professional transcribers. During the data analysis process, we removed interviewees' identities and assigned each of them a pseudonym. We analyzed the transcribed data and summarized the emerging themes.

Factors Facilitating Women's IT Career Choice

Building upon previous discussion, the following section further summarizes how individual characteristics may influence female students' success in IT program at Iowa community colleges. The interview data revealed that assertive personality and characteristics of nontraditional students are two factors that worth to be mentioned.

Assertive Personality.   All interviewees observed personal and social factors that drove women to choose an IT major and eventually an IT profession. The first factor refers to women's personality traits where many interviewees mentioned "personality" as one of the reasons why some women would be successful in IT. For example, Sophie, a female faculty member in IT, indicated that there are "assertive" women and not so "assertive" women in her class. She described them as follows:

> Some of them are strong and come up to the front and assert themselves. I don't see that quite probably as often as some that are still hanging back and seeing what can I do.... The assertive ones, they are taken a lot better than the ones that aren't quite so assertive. I think helping them to get their self-esteem or helping them to somehow feel like they have just as much to contribute, maybe, is difficult.

Teresa, another female faculty member in IT, described female students who she thought were more competent than others.

> [Interviewer: What is it about them that made you feel they were competent, that they could do this?] Coming in from high school, and then also their GPAs, and also their personalities I think, and the way that they spoke. They didn't seem like they were lost; they seemed like they were driven, that they had a goal.

Nontraditional Student.   Many of the IT students are working adults who seek job promotion or mothers who want to return to the workforce. It was interesting to discover several interviewees advocate their nontraditional students' open mindset and initiative. Faculty members and administrators often noticed that nontraditional women tend to have more life experiences and are strongly motivated. Judy, a female district IT program coordinator, shared a life story of a female student.

> We've had working mothers who came back. I had one that was a photographer, she came back and went through the programming degree. She was hired at a very, ..., very good company in the [city name] and has just

blossomed in her career. Then, now she does her photography on the side. She still has a love for photography but she really is very good in the coding area. Unfortunately, in the middle of all this she got a divorce, but now she's able to support herself and her son because she now has a job that allows her to do that.

The other interviewees also shared that nontraditional women would have a clearer vision of what they need and what opportunities are available in the IT workforce. For example, a female faculty member, Sara, talked about one of her nontraditional students:

> that's what I would have thought was for Madeline, it was there are jobs here and there's money to be made there. It's not that she had any great love of computers or anything.

Exemplary Practices of Recruiting and Retaining Women in IT

The following section discusses exemplary practices of recruiting and retaining women in community college IT programs. In particular, recruiting programs, classroom strategies, mentoring system and role models are four practices that interviewees shared.

Recruiting Programs.   The three community colleges had recruiting programs pertaining to attracting students to their IT programs. Specifically, the two IT coordinators shared their particular recruiting programs.

Grace, one of the IT coordinators, shared the experiences in High Tech Girls Day, a recruiting program specifically targeting young females. Grace highlighted the main focus of the program is to build up girls' confidence within a supportive environment.

> We have a High Tech Girls Day and a High Tech Guys Day. The reason we separate it, and for many years it was just High Tech Girls Day to encourage that group of students, ... we've done it separated because it gives young females, we target the ages of 8th through 12th graders, the confidence with a group of their peers to not feel embarrassed if they don't know something or they can work through things together, and be creative or helpful for each other. It's just a very supportive atmosphere and environment for young females.

Compared to Grace's college, Judy's college hosted an event called Plant Yourself in STEM involves the participation from the local Girl Scouts. Judy believed that the representation from women in IT inspired many young women who attended the event to imagine themselves in IT area in the future.

Strategies in the Classroom.   When interviewing faculty members, many classroom strategies for engaging female students were mentioned. For example, Sophie, an IT faculty member, noticed that one of her female students, Alice, tended to be more comfortable in a smaller group. She described Alice's experiences in her class in detail.

> I'm looking at Alice now, just Alice. When she was in the group of five, she was pushed to a backseat or taking a backseat where she's, "Well, what can I do?" and took whatever was left over rather than being more assertive. As that class got smaller and smaller and smaller, it was a one-on-one, her and Brett. Robert's military, and he's very stiff with her; boom, boom, boom. Those two excelled very well. Alice did very well working in that group, and she was very successful in that group. It was one-on-one. She worked in groups of three and she worked in groups of five, and the more guys she was with it seemed like the more toward the backseat she went.

A common strategies that favor female students is keeping the class size small. In all of the interviews, interviewees agreed that a small class size is critical for facilitating women's success in IT.

Supportive Mentoring System.   All interviewees highlighted the importance of having a supportive mentoring system that consisted of faculty members, academic advisors, career counselors, and other administrators. Interviewees directly or indirectly advocated the necessity of building a systematic support environment, either formally or informally. Faculty members need to be "approachable" and academic advisors need to be "dedicated." The career counselors should serve as the bridge between the industry and the community college and provide the most suitable advice to female students. It needs to be a group effort. Creating a welcoming environment that makes women feel like they are "fitting in" is the goal. One of the interviewees described the informal mentoring system as follows:

> We do have an informal mentoring system because we do have a lot of female instructors and adjunct instructors. I guess maybe that helps. Maybe that informal mentoring with them. Any advising role, we help them select their classes. We're asking them what kind of things do you need? We've done it really informally.

Role Models.   In accordance with previous studies, our interviewees recognized the positive impact of role models and provided many experiences with establishing role models for female students. For example, all interviewees highlighted the female faculty members and administrator representations at their community colleges. Furthermore, interviewees' community colleges intentionally provide female role models in other formats, such as speakers at various events. Grace's college, for instance, invited a female speaker to a recruiting event. Grace thought the speaker was "phenomenal."

The speaker last year I cannot say enough about. She was absolutely phe-nomenal. She works for a company, she's actually in marketing, but yet she works for a company just up the road here in [city name]. She was local. She talked about how girls can get involved in IT and how easy it is, and there's IT everywhere that you see. It was a very successful year for us.

Challenges of Recruiting and Retaining Women in IT

The following section presents challenges pertaining to recruiting and re-taining female students in community college IT programs. Specifically, the interviewees shared three types of individual challenges that female stu-dents in IT programs often face. Further, interview data indicates that the lack of institutional data is a major organizational challenge.

Individual Challenges of Women in IT.   Based on their observation, interviewees concluded three types of challenges the individual female IT student is facing. The first one centers on women's confidence levels regard-ing IT. During the interviews, multiple female faculty members mentioned that the lack of confidence has prevented female students from better per-forming in the class. The following quote represented what the interviewees have observed from their daily experiences.

When they're working in teams in seems like . . . We do have several strong females but most of the time the females do not take on that leadership role and do not experiment with that leadership role. We do have a class on lead-ership and professionalism which is kind of forcing everyone to see what it's like to be a leader, to take on that leadership role and to maybe reflect on their skills that they could bring to the table in a leadership role. They're just a little more hesitant to do that, maybe not quite as confident in their skills. That's one thing we find in the job interviews too is they're not as confident. They are skilled, they know what they're doing but they lack confidence.

The second student-level challenge is from family obligations. Child care, financial issues, and time conflicts often prohibit women from devot-ing more time and energy to their studies. Whereas the first type of chal-lenges can apply to all female students, this second one is especially true for the nontraditional female students. A direct consequence for nontra-ditional female students is that they may miss classes due to these obli-gations. During the faculty focus group interview, interviewees provided examples. In particular, a female student may not be able to attend a class because "the workmen are still at my house. They were supposed to have left but they are still here so I can't come to class today." Also, a mom may miss a class because "the school is closed and I don't have a babysitter for my kid."

A third challenge can be applied not only to female students but to all students in IT. Faculty members and administrators highlighted the lack of academic preparedness in terms of math, writing, and speaking as a challenge for students. The IT program coordinator, Grace, described that the math challenges the students have had caused the program to adjust their curriculum.

> One thing we did … is really re-evaluated math. Math is challenging for students in this program. We re-evaluated really what we need our graduates to actually [be], in turn, end up lowering, slightly not significantly, but lowering slightly, the standard to graduate for math in our area, or for this program. … we have had some students take math classes for 4 or 5 semesters, failing or retaking or whatever it may be, and so we're hoping that will change that.

The other general skills, namely, writing and speaking, were also mentioned by Grace as a challenge to IT students. Although these communication skills are highly recommended by employers, students are often negatively influenced by the stereotype that IT students are not good at speaking and writing. Sometime students even "moan and groan" when they realized that they have to take a communication class.

Lack of Institutional Data.   Except for some uncertainties in implementing their plans, the interviewees did not express too many concerns about challenges at the organizational level. However, although not explicitly addressed, there were organizational-level challenges that interviewees are facing in their daily work. One of them is the lack of data support. Specifically, Grace, the IT program coordinator, mentioned multiple times that she does not have enough data to back up her statements. For example, when asked how many female students are enrolled in her program overall, Grace indicated that 17% of female students enrolled in computer support specialist program. She indicated that, however, she did not have data for the female enrollment in all IT programs. Similarly, Grace noticed that nontraditional female students were facing additional difficulties including not being able to attend class full time. However, she implied that it was merely her observation and was not sure if there were statistics to support her conclusions. Allowing administrators and front-line practitioners free access to necessary data may require an institutional or even regional effort. The contribution from institutional research offices or third-party researchers may be essential to facilitate the data literacy building among the community.

Recommendations

Our work explored some exemplary practices and challenges of recruiting and retaining women in IT programs in the Iowa community college context. The interviews with the IT program administrators and faculty members provided valuable information to community college educators and practitioners who recognize the gender issues in the IT workforce.

First of all, our analysis highlighted the effectiveness of targeting women in community college recruiting programs. There are at least two approaches that community colleges may use to attract and engage potential female students in IT programs. First, community colleges may design special recruiting events for females. Such events can group young females together and create a stress-free, supportive environment for potential students. Also, these recruiting events can provide female students opportunities to connect with female faculty members, counselors, advisors, and leaders who are working within an IT program. A small, intimate atmosphere may facilitate the communication among educators and future students. In the second approach, community colleges can invite local organizations such as the Girl Scouts to regular recruiting events. Inviting local organizations to recruiting events may be more cost effective than hosting events specially designed for potential female students. Additionally, it is important for the event coordinators to include working females and mothers in the target pool. These women may have different interests and needs compared to younger females. The recruiting event coordinators should be mindful of the nontraditional student's unique needs and develop the recruiting events accordingly.

Second, community college IT program educators and practitioners need to be aware of characteristics of nontraditional female students as adult learners and provide support for them throughout their education. For example, some adult females usually struggle with child care, part-time jobs, and other family obligations. It might be helpful to develop a more flexible class schedule for them. Some effective strategies may include individualized class time, extended open hours for labs, and online learning modules. It is also necessary to provide a flexible advisor and counselor schedule to further engage adult women.

In accordance with previous research, our interviewees emphasized the importance of role models in promoting women's success in IT. It is important, therefore, that community college IT programs keep providing female role models to their students. One way to provide female role models to students is to expand the female representation within the program. Another way is to bring successful female IT professionals to students through workshops, seminars, and invited forums.

Last but not the least, it is imperative to have researchers and evaluators conduct empirical work based on an institution's activity in recruiting and retaining women in IT. Both institutional research offices and third-party researchers may lead such studies and evaluations. It is the institution's responsibility to obtain the results and make it accessible to all IT program educators and practitioners. A regional organization may facilitate this process by encouraging institutional studies, maintaining regional data-sharing platforms, and hosting regional research conferences.

References

Ahuja, M. (2002). Women in the information technology profession: A literature review, synthesis and research agenda. *European Journal of Information Systems, 11*, 20–34.

Bailey, T., Alfonso, M., Scott, M., & Leinbach, T. (2004). *Education outcomes of occupational postsecondary students.* Report prepared for the National Assessment of Vocational Education, U.S. Department of Education. Retrieved from http://ccrc.tc.columbia.edu/publications/educational-outcomes-occupational-postsecondary-students.html

Hill, C., Corbett, C., & St. Rose, A. (2010). *Why so few? Women in science, technology, engineering, and mathematics.* Washington, DC: American Association of University Women. Retrieved from http://www.aauw.org/research/why-so-few/

Iowa Department of Education. (2014a). *The annual condition of Iowa's community colleges 2014.* Retrieved from https://www.educateiowa.gov/documents/condition-community-colleges/2015/01/annual-condition-iowas-community-colleges-2014

Iowa Department of Education. (2014b). *Education outcomes: Certificate, diploma, and associate programs, Iowa Community Colleges FY 2010 to FY 2012.* Retrieved from https://www.educateiowa.gov/sites/files/ed/documents/Community%20College%20Program%20Report.pdf

Iowa Department of Education. (2014c). *2014 community college fall enrollment report.* Retrieved from https://www.educateiowa.gov/documents/fall-enrollment/2014/11/2014-community-college-fall-enrollment-report

Lester, L. (2010). Women in male-dominated career and technical education programs at community colleges: Barriers to participation and success. *Journal of Women and Minorities in Science and Engineering, 16*(1), 51–66.

Lockard, C. B., & Wolf, M. (2012). Occupational employment projections to 2020. *Monthly Labor Review, 135*(1), 84–108. Retrieved from http://www.bls.gov/opub/mlr/2012/01/art5full.pdf

Mooney, G. M., & Foley, D. J. (2011). *Community colleges: Playing an important role in the education of science, engineering, and health graduates* (Info-Brief NSF11-317). Arlington, VA: National Science Foundation. Retrieved from http://www.nsf.gov/statistics/infbrief/nsf11317/

National Center for Women & Information Technology. (2014). *NCWIT scorecard: A report on the status of women in information technology.* Retrieved from http://www.ncwit.org/scorecard

National Science Foundation & National Center for Science and Engineering Statistics. (2015). *Women, minorities, and persons with disabilities in science and engineering* (Special Report NSF 15-311). Retrieved from http://www.nsf.gov/statistics/wmpd/

Richards, E., & Terkanian, D. (2013). Occupational employment projections to 2022. *Monthly Labor Review.* Retrieved from http://www.bls.gov/opub/mlr/2013/article/occupational-employment-projections-to-2022-1.htm

Spencer, S. J., Steele, C. M., & Quinn, D. M., (1999). Stereotype threat and women's math performance. *Journal of Experimental Social Psychology, 35*(1), 4–28.

Trauth, E. M. (2002). Odd girl out: An individual differences perspective on women in the IT profession. *Information Technology and People, 15*(2), 98–118.

Trauth, E. M., & Howcroft, D. (2006). Critical empirical research in IS: An example of gender and IT. *Information Technology and People, Special Issus on Critical Research in Information Systems, 19*(3), 272–292.

Trauth, E. M., Quesenberry, J. L., & Huang, H. (2008). A multicultural analysis of factors influencing career choice for women in the information technology workforce. *Journal of Global Information Management, 16*(4), 1–23.

Tsapogas, J. (2004). *The role of community college in the education of recent science and engineering graduates* (Info Brief NSF 04-315). Arlington, VA: National Science Foundation.

NEW DIRECTIONS FOR COMMUNITY COLLEGES • DOI: 10.1002/cc

Turner, S. V., Bernt, P. W., & Pecora, N. (2002). Why Women Choose Information Technology Careers: Educational, Social, and Familial Influences. Paper presented at the Annual Meeting of the American Educational Research Association, New Orleans, LA. Retrieved from https://eric.ed.gov/?id=ED465878

U.S. Census Bureau. (2014). *Annual estimates of the resident population by sex, race and Hispanic origin for the United States, and counties: April 1, 2010 to July 1, 2014.* Retrieved from https://factfinder.census.gov/faces/tableservices/jsf/pages/productview.xhtml?src=bkmk

YU (APRIL) CHEN *is a postdoctoral research fellow in the School of Education at Iowa State University.*

ARLENE DE LA MORA *is a research scientist in Research Institute for Studies in Education at Iowa State University.*

MARI KEMIS *is the interim director of Research Institute for Studies in Education at Iowa State University.*

NEW DIRECTIONS FOR COMMUNITY COLLEGES • DOI: 10.1002/cc

8

This chapter provides a summary of the aforementioned chapters and includes implications for policy and practice and lessons for the future as it relates to CTE programs and STEM education.

Implications for Policy and Practice: Summary of the Volume and Lessons for the Future of CTE Programs and STEM

Dimitra Jackson Smith

Career and technical education (CTE) programs are at the forefront of leading the charge in preparing a competent STEM workforce. The contents of this issue highlight three significant areas related to the role of CTE programs in preparing a STEM economic workforce, which includes (a) incorporating experiential learning activities for students in CTE programs, (b) providing avenues and effective strategies for closing the skills gap for students in CTE through funding and evaluation and assessment activities, and (c) highlighting the experiences of women in CTE programs. The implications for policy and practice will focus around these three tenets.

Experiential learning strategies and approaches are not new to CTE programs. In fact, according to Clark, Threeton, and Ewing (2010), "experiential learning has been a major component of career and technical education for many years" (para 2). Experiential learning was referred to by many terms in this issue including applied learning and hands-on learning. The authors in this book go on to suggest that even with this experiential component to CTE programs, the actual implementation of experiential learning and hands-on approaches within context is unclear, disconnected, and not support or well informed by research. Wang, Wang, and Prevost (Chapter 2) propose that applied learning components that engage the researcher, the practitioner, and the data in the academic learning process be fully incorporated into CTE programs. The authors took a particular focus on the area of remedial math. Given the large number of students who enter community colleges underprepared in math and the even larger percentage of individuals who lack the necessary skills to obtain math- and

NEW DIRECTIONS FOR COMMUNITY COLLEGES, no. 178, Summer 2017 © 2017 Wiley Periodicals, Inc.
Published online in Wiley Online Library (wileyonlinelibrary.com) • DOI: 10.1002/cc.20256

science-related careers, many students are not positioned to be successful in CTE programs.

The authors advise that in developing innovative transformed remedial math programs, partnerships are essential in linking "a diverse family of instructional strategies designed to more seamlessly link the learning of foundational skills and academic or occupational content by focusing teaching and learning squarely on concrete applications in a specific context that is of interest to the student" (Mazzeo, 2008, p. 3). Funded by the Advanced Technological Education (ATE) program of the National Science Foundation, Wang, Wang, and Prevost developed a project focused on improving student success within manufacturing engineering technologist and technician education (METTE) programs at Wisconsin's 2-year colleges. When many of their students were underprepared in math, members involved in the researcher–practitioner partnership began to explore innovations in math learning and teaching for underprepared students. The authors recommend that the researcher–practitioner partnership, with each using their areas of expertise, center around creating and using high-quality data to understand who CTE students are and what skills they need to acquire to be successful in CTE-related careers.

In Chapter 3, Edgar Troudt, Stuart Schulman, and Christoph Winkler concur with the use of applied learning strategies that includes partnerships and highlight a very specific experiential learning strategy, which they refer to as a Virtual Enterprise (VE). The authors discussed a very detailed VE, operated as an active learning pedagogical system, which allows students the opportunity to simulate the conceptualization and operation of an entrepreneurial business start-up inside a classroom. Beginning as a fully standalone business education course and operating in the mode of an internship, the entrepreneurship simulation taught basic business operation techniques and professional skills. The authors agree that the pedagogical system is training and labor intensive and often requires the participation of partners. They suggest systematizing training through a series of videos that incorporates the processes that students commence in their classroom. These videos will be useful not only to students but also to faculty members, administrators, and instructors. For students, the videos will demonstrate model business and entrepreneurial activities that the students will assume in the classroom. For faculty members, administrators, and instructors, the video will guide them through how to incorporate entrepreneurial activities and exercises into STEM classrooms. In allowing for the application of the pedagogical system into other disciplines and other educational situations, the authors suggest crowdsourcing through commission action research studies.

The inclusion of experiential learning techniques continues to be an avenue for CTE programs to prepare a competent STEM workforce. Experiential learning strategies allow students to move past merely learning and engaging in textbook information but ceasing the opportunity to take this learning and apply it in real-world, authentic context in classrooms. The chance to engage in such application activities allow students to work through challenges and gain viable skills in a safe, controlled environment. Researcher–practitioner partnerships in academic courses, such as remedial math and partner relationships in simulation activities, are several ways that the workforce can be brought into the classroom environment.

CTE programs can also prepare a competent workforce by providing innovative ways to close the skills gap. This issue discusses two ways that CTE programs can close the skills gap through funding innovations and program measurement and evaluation. Research indicates that the incorporation of collaborative funding streams that encourages collaboration, alignment, and the ability for a student to transition between secondary and postsecondary systems are essential to student preparedness and student success (Brown, 2003). Community colleges serve a large portion of our prospective workforce population. Coupled with this is the fact that the majority of CTE programs require advanced technologies and equipment to ensure students have relevant instruction and up-to-date laboratory experiences that are needed in many of our nation's high-demand career pathways. Even with this, external funding for community colleges has not kept pace with funding at 4-year institutions (Century Foundation Task Force, 2013). For example, the authors highlight the American Graduation Initiative (AGI), which promised to invest roughly 12 billion dollars in community colleges over 10 years; instead the community college initiative was reduced to an investment of only 2 billion dollars into community colleges in funds managed by the U.S. Department of Labor to help dislocated workers access training programs. There are, however, some promising funding allocations through external sources through the Department of Labor, NSF, and the Department of Education to name a few as well as through corporate and private foundations, such as J.P. Morgan Chase.

Although strides have been made to level the field of institutional funding through industry partnerships and career funds, innovative strategies must be incorporated. Lowry and Thomas-Anderson (Chapter 4) found through research that "2-year colleges have been least likely to serve as recipients of external funding opportunities to develop and implement funding programs commonly offered by agencies as intramural and/or extramural funding." Although workforce development is typically funded through three types of revenue sources, which include (a) funds that are included as part of the state appropriation to community colleges, (b) additional funding outlined for community colleges to use in support of workforce development, and (c) nonstate funding sources, Lowry and Thomas-Anderson argue that community college budgets rarely include funds to support projects designed to enhance research and/or programs of study in career and technical education internally. In addressing this gap, the authors shed light on the need to identify secondary funding sources and/or encourage partnerships.

Innovative strategies for ensuring the success of CTE programs and students has been identified; however, these programs and improvement strategies must be linked to program evaluation to ensure the outcomes, both stated and implied, are reasonable and just for all students, specifically for underserved students. Federal policies and regulations such as the 2006 amended Perkins Vocational Act has enhanced the development and funding of vocational education programs. As mentioned by Lowry and Thomas-Anderson and further elaborated by Bragg in Chapter 5, funding is a significant factor in the success of women and additional special populations. Unfortunately, the flexibility provided to funding institutions results in high-poverty districts not benefiting from increased funding as more affluent areas and districts do. In response to the ensuring that more equitable student outcomes are produced by CTE programs, Bragg assisted in the development of a program evaluation and continuous improvement process for career pathways and programs called Pathways to Results (PTR). In short, PTR focuses on leadership and support for improvement, assessment of student access and improvement, alignment among education and training, enhanced learning, completion and credential attainment, comprehensive professional development, and data collection. Although PTR is linear in nature, Bragg highlights the importance of entering the PTR process in a way that seems appropriate for specific programs. Additional information regarding the PTR program is in Chapter 6.

Last, when highlighting innovative strategies and the role of funding and program evaluation in student success, it is essential to take into account the impact of gender, more specifically the experiences of women in the classroom environment. According to Lester, Struthers, and Yamanaka (Chapter 6), ensuring that pedagogy and peer interactions in classroom environments are positive and conducive to the success of women in CTE programs could have a positive impact on their experiences. Through an ethnographic case study, Lester et al. unveiled three microinvalidations that affect the decision of women to pursue a STEM-related career path. These microinvalidations include a consistent pattern of female isolation across all CTE courses, a competitive classroom environment with few interactions, and gendered language. Through interviews and focus groups, Chen, Kemis, and de la Mora (Chapter 7) highlight the gender imbalance of IT programs in Iowa community colleges. The authors shed light on specific recommendations for recruiting and retaining women in IT-related career paths. According to the authors, community colleges are positioned to lead the charge and can develop special recruiting events and programs for females as well as invite local organizations to regular recruiting events. The authors further highlight the need to be aware of characteristics that are specific to nontraditional female students.

In closing, the success of students, including women in CTE programs is the responsibility of all individuals who work directly and indirectly with students in CTE programs. As previously mentioned, CTE programs are leading the charge in STEM preparation. Provided this essential role of CTE programs, ensuring clear and comprehensive pathways to the STEM workforce, fostering environments conducive to student success through math and science preparation and hands on simulation activities are necessary. Additionally, a particular focus should be on the role of microaggressions and unwelcoming classroom environments. As educational environments are further improved for students in CTE programs, providing multiple streams of funding and funding innovations as well as evaluating student outcomes and equity gaps will ensure that students are able to successfully navigate through CTE programs into the STEM workforce.

References

Brown, B. L. (2003). *Connecting CTE to labor market information*. Columbus, OH: Ohio State University, Center on Education and Training for Employment. Retrieved from ERIC database. (ED479341).

Century Foundation Taskforce of Preventing Community Colleges from Becoming Separate and Unequal. (2013). *Bridging the higher education divide: Strengthening community colleges and restoring the American dream*. New York, NY: Century Foundation Press.

Clark, R. W., Threeton, M. D., & Ewing, J. C. (2010). The potential of experiential learning models and practices in career and technical education & career and technical teacher education. *Journal of Career and Technical Education, 25*(2).

Mazzeo, C. (2008). *Supporting student success at California community colleges: A white paper*. Prepared for the Bay Area Workforce Funding Collaborative Career by the Career Ladders Project for California Community Colleges.

DIMITRA JACKSON *Smith is a tenured associate professor in the Department of Educational Psychology and Leadership (Higher Education Program) at Texas Tech University in Lubbock, Texas.*

INDEX

NEW DIRECTIONS FOR COMMUNITY COLLEGE
ORDER FORM SUBSCRIPTION AND SINGLE ISSUES

DISCOUNTED BACK ISSUES:

Use this form to receive 20% off all back issues of *New Directions for Community College*.
All single issues priced at **$23.20** (normally $29.00)

TITLE   ISSUE NO.   ISBN

_____   _____   _____
_____   _____   _____
_____   _____   _____

*Call 1-800-835-6770 or see mailing instructions below. When calling, mention the promotional code JBNND to receive
your discount. For a complete list of issues, please visit www.wiley.com/WileyCDA/WileyTitle/productCd-CC.html*

SUBSCRIPTIONS: (1 YEAR, 4 ISSUES)

☐ New Order   ☐ Renewal

U.S.	☐ Individual: $89	☐ Institutional: $356
CANADA/MEXICO	☐ Individual: $89	☐ Institutional: $398
ALL OTHERS	☐ Individual: $113	☐ Institutional: $434

*Call 1-800-835-6770 or see mailing and pricing instructions below.
Online subscriptions are available at www.onlinelibrary.wiley.com*

ORDER TOTALS:

Issue / Subscription Amount: $ _____

Shipping Amount: $ _____
(for single issues only – subscription prices include shipping)

Total Amount: $ _____

SHIPPING CHARGES:

First Item $6.00
Each Add'l Item $2.00

*(No sales tax for U.S. subscriptions. Canadian residents, add GST for subscription orders. Individual rate subscriptions must
be paid by personal check or credit card. Individual rate subscriptions may not be resold as library copies.)*

BILLING & SHIPPING INFORMATION:

☐ **PAYMENT ENCLOSED:** *(U.S. check or money order only. All payments must be in U.S. dollars.)*

☐ **CREDIT CARD:** ☐ VISA ☐ MC ☐ AMEX

Card number _____ Exp. Date_____

Card Holder Name_____ Card Issue # _____

Signature _____ Day Phone_____

☐ **BILL ME:** *(U.S. institutional orders only. Purchase order required.)*

Purchase order # _____
                 Federal Tax ID 13559302 • GST 89102-8052

Name_____

Address_____

Phone_____ E-mail_____

Copy or detach page and send to: **John Wiley & Sons, Inc. / Jossey Bass
PO Box 55381
Boston, MA 02205-9850**

PROMO JBNND